This book belongs to Dawn Luebbe

19 92 *to* 19 92

TABLE OF CONTENTS

Introduction 6

Chapter One: Attempts to Be Cool 12

Chapter Two: Passion On the Prairie 35

Chapter Three: Remembering the '90s 58

Chapter Four: Untalented:
   A Collection of Failed Hobbies 78

Chapter Five: Preteen Conflict:
   The Art of Overreaction 96

Chapter Six: Tato Skins, TCBY, and Trix:
   A Sophisticated Palate 118

Chapter Seven: Nebraska: Horses,
   Tornados, and Casseroles 137

Chapter Eight: Growing Pains 150

Epilogue 168

Acknowledgments 172

About the Author 173

My Diary

INTRODUCTION

Perhaps you think you're about to peer into the life of an incredibly popular, smart, and cute preteen. Perhaps you're anticipating the Kelly Kapowski of Lincoln, Nebraska—a talented and pretty girl all the boys adored. Perhaps you're expecting someone who could spell the word "choir."

If so, you are about to be considerably disappointed.

Like most girls, I entered what you might consider an awkward phase around the age of nine. Unlike most girls, I remained there for well over a decade—a decade during which people stopped looking at me with expressions of joy and endearment and gazed upon my gawky form with pity and mild distaste.

Let's start with my looks. At eleven, I was already a head taller than my friends, and though I love being tall now, being a giantess in fifth grade is like being a Misfit at a Jem concert. Despite my best efforts to stunt my growth with a steady diet of Doritos and Dairy Queen, I always towered over my classmates.

In addition to giving André the Giant a run for his money, I was also skinny. Not skinny in a fit, attractive kind of way, but skinny in a "my stretch pants are baggy" kind of way. Think Jack Skellington with Rollerblades and a perm.

And even though I was tall, I was an intensely late bloomer. Despite praying for boobs every night, every morning I'd wake up, look in the mirror, and stare with disappointment at my concave chest. Apparently God had better things to do.

Glasses were a required part of my wardrobe from early on. Rather than go with a simple, understated tortoiseshell, I took my inspiration from Sally Jessy Raphael—a fashion role model to *all* children—and opted for a bold frame: turquoise.

Though I didn't wear braces until my junior year (the perfect look for prom), I was into wearing *pretend* braces, i.e., an unfolded paper clip placed atop my front teeth. I can only assume I was the inspiration for grills. You're welcome, Lil Wayne.

Completing my style were curly, overly hair-sprayed bangs that evoked a look best described as electrocution-chic.

But I was a modern preteen, and I didn't rely on my looks alone to get by. I also relied on my coolness. I dazzled family and friends by writing and performing raps and choreographing dances to Paula Abdul hits. (As the resident family badass, I played MC Skat Kat while my sister Ginger was Paula.)

But the acts of coolness didn't stop there. I dominated my suburban neighborhood atop my splatter-painted Huffy mountain bike. I entered our school's lip-sync contest with "Motownphilly." I wore my overalls with one strap down. I was pushing the coolness meter to its breaking point.

The setting of my tween trials and tribulations was the "Paris of the Midwest": Lincoln, Nebraska, and its surrounding suburbs (OK, farms). A Midwestern upbringing—don't be jealous—is *exceptional*. It involved sewing glamorous fuchsia pantsuits for 4-H competitions, throwing snowballs at unsuspecting cows on my grandparents' farm, dining on casseroles and pop for supper, and assuming that all people fell into two religious factions: Evangelical Lutheran or Missouri Synod Lutheran.

My family was what you might consider a typical family, though perhaps with slightly more coordinated outfits.

My pesky brother, Tom, performed his older-brother duties admirably by ~~protecting and mentoring me~~ being a huge annoyance. Whether he was reading my diary or stealing my hard-earned Halloween candy, he was always bugging me. But with his neon bike shorts and dancing Coke can, I couldn't help but secretly admit he was pretty cool.

My sister, Ginger, one year my junior, was the baby of the family, but she was smarter and more talented than the rest of us combined. When not playing Balloon Girl in the Lincoln Community Playhouse's production of *Gypsy*, she could be found in an advanced swimming class or solving math problems for fun.

My father, Larry, poured concrete by day and was the ultimate mustachioed grill master by night. He also saw to it that my siblings and I were exposed to Nebraska's finest cultural event—car racing at Eagle Raceway.

My mother, Diane, a part-time travel agent and full-time fashionista, was my inspiration when it came to style (aside from Sally Jessy, of course). Whether she was sporting her BeDazzled denim jumpsuit or her shoulder-length earrings, she always had it going on.

It was also my mom who, on a recent trip to our basement to stow her lavender cowboy boots, discovered my 1990–1992 diaries. After prying off the locks, I was surprised at what was inside. I had completely forgotten about the report I did on Rudy Huxtable for Black History Month. I barely remember the time I played a camel in our church's live Nativity. And I suspect I am still blocking out any recollection of the time I threw up at Six Flags. But my diaries reminded me of all these precious moments.

I shared these diaries with some friends who also happened to be preteens in the early '90s, and I found they could totally relate. They, too, thought Brandon Walsh was a hunk. They, too, rocked out to Marky Mark and the Funky Bunch. They, too, were obsessed with *WWF Prime Time Wrestling*. (OK, maybe that last one was just me.)

Reassured that I was not the only one who hoarded trolls and rocked stonewashed Z. Cavariccis, I decided to share these entries with a wider audience through a Tumblr blog, which lead to this book. The following are actual pages of my preteen diaries, unedited, uncensored, and very, very un-spell-checked.

So put on your parachute pants, turn up your Gloria Estefan, grab a can of Jolt, and enjoy.

Chapter 1

ATTEMPTS TO BE COOL

I'd like to think I had lofty goals at age eleven, such as bettering myself intellectually, being a nicer person, and contributing to society. But, frankly, I had one objective—achieving coolness. I knew this was my ticket to securing a boyfriend and gaining popularity (the only important things on Earth).

Strutting through the halls of Julius Humann Elementary in my turquoise vest and hot pink Keds, my wrist laden with friendship bracelets (from myself), I knew I was on the right track.

I had plenty of A-list role models to look to for inspiration: Shannen Doherty for her looks and bad-girl reputation, Janet Jackson for her sassiness and incredible dance moves, and Smurfette, who simply had it all.

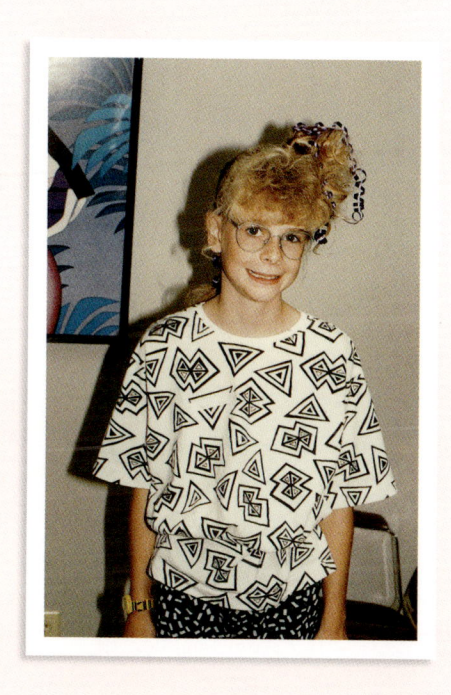

Chapter 1

Early-'90s preteen popularity was measured by one primary barometer: bangs height. If you wanted to figure out who the most popular girl was, all you had to do was look for the highest wall of hair.

This is Sarah, one of the most popular girls at Humann Elementary in 1992:

Feast your eyes on the work of art perched above her forehead. This was the dream. Her bangs literally did not move. And they had staying power. They were just as high at the end of the school day as they were in homeroom. Sarah was a bangs master. She was the girl everyone wanted to be.

My bangs—*ahem*—were a little more unwieldy:

Believe it or not, that's a photo of them looking their best.

Like the mighty peacock's tail, the height and feathering of your bangs determined your place in the hair hierarchy.

Bangs preparation was a time-consuming and precarious act. The hair wizard's tool, the curling iron, had to be at just the right temperature, and the curl had to be held for the perfect amount of time. You knew you were on the right track when a trace amount of steam rose from the iron as it charred the hair spray. Things could quickly go awry, however. If you clamped down too abruptly, your bangs would crease in an angular, unnatural style. If you didn't hold the curl long enough, you'd get flat bangs, and you might as well just stay home from school.

Chapter 1

The amount of hair spray (my magic elixir was Aussie) was key. Too little, and your bangs would be flat by lunchtime; too much, and they would become dark and crunchy, collapsing under their own immense weight. I often had a very heavy hand when it came to hair spray, as evidenced by this entry from May 31, 1992.

Ever the cultural sponge, I made a trip to see *The Sound of Music* at the Lincoln Community Playhouse. Looking back, I can only feel sorry for the unfortunate soul seated behind me who had to strain his or her neck to get a view of the von Trapp children over my tower of bangs.

After the show we cruised downtown to the ultimate '90s dessert mecca, TCBY. Nothing drowns the sorrow of imperfect bangs like the sweet tang of frozen yogurt. I was usually a Dairy Queen girl myself, but TCBY was on the menu when my mom went on one of her health kicks. If we spotted Mom in the den doing aerobics to her Jane Fonda workout record, we knew it was TCBY for us.

Sunday
MAY 31

Today I spent 20 minutes on my bangs! I had to ~~~~ wash dishes. At about 12:45 we went to the library, then we went to see the sound of music at the Cummunity Playhouse!! It was so good! Then we went to TCBY! Tonight I watched T.V.

P.S.= My bangs had tons of hairspray on my bangs.

— Dawn

Apparently the hairspray fumes had reached my brain by the time I wrote the postscript.

Chapter __1__

I was *very* serious about my bangs. So serious, in fact, that not even clarinet practice or the latest episode of *Beverly Hills, 90210* could distract me from the disaster atop my head. The time had come to take action. I needed to grow them out.

Under the impression that all matters of appearance fell under my mother's purview, I sought her approval on this important style choice. I was sure she would be in favor of it. After all, my mom truly embodied style and sophistication. I mean, seriously, look at her:

I was certain she would take one look at the hair-sprayed nest on my forehead and say, "Of course you should grow those out!" But that was not what she said. No, her response was so devastating that it led me to issue a suicide threat (punctuated by a frowning face).

Thursday JANUARY 9

Today we changed the scudule around at school. It's a ok. scedule. After school I went to dance, it was fun. After Dance, we came home, ate, then I practiced my clarinet. Then mom went to some other important meeting. I watched 90210. When mom got home I asked her a question I had been ding to ask her for about 2 years. "Can I grow my bangs out?". She said "Well you would have to cut your hair so short to match your bangs." NOT!!! no one else dose!

P.S.= Sometimes I want to die! Dawn!

Chapter 1

Fortunately, I survived the bangs tragedy (though certainly a changed woman). I eventually moved on and focused on other things—namely, discovering cool new music.

By the early '90s, rap music had entered the mainstream. No wading in the kiddie pool for me; I went straight into the deep end: Will Smith's "Parents Just Don't Understand." Not only was it the greatest music video I had seen since "Walk Like an Egyptian," it was also something I could definitely relate to. Like Will Smith, *my* parents just didn't understand. (Need I remind you about the recent bangs debacle?!)

Another rap that inspired me was "Do the Bartman" by Bart Simpson. I had a huge crush on Bart, and I wasn't going to let the fact that he was animated get in the way. Skateboarders were my weakness, especially skateboarders with number one rap singles.

Inspired by Will and Bart, I entered the freestyle scene myself, via the postscript of this entry. My rap begins with a topic I knew a lot about as the grandchild of a dairy farmer: milk. But my wholesome rhyme soon takes a violent turn. Forget the East Coast/West Coast feud, the real rap war was born in the Midwest.

Sunday
JANUARY 26

This morning I woke up at Grandma & Grandpa Luebbe's house. We went to church. After church we went to a soup. Then we went back to G&G's house for an hour. Then we drove to our house to watch the super bowl 26. The Redskins won. For supper we ordered in mcdonalds. The P.S. is a rap I wrote.

P.S. = I went to the store to buy a carton of milk, who do you think was there but Mr. Bilk. He asked me for a quarter, I said "No way", he punched me in the stomach & I said "HEY"!!

Dawn!!!

In a rare entry with no spelling errors, I didn't want to jinx things by attempting to spell out the Roman numerals for 26.

Chapter **1**

Everyone knows that the greatest rappers aren't afraid to drop a dirty word on occasion. If I was ever going to compete with 2Pac and Heavy D, I needed to acquire some new vocabulary. Unfortunately, cursing was an absolute no-no in our family. Even the mildest curses, like "that sucks" or "oh, crap," would get you sent to your room. Thus, it was important to disguise your curse words.

On February 11, 1992, my cursing came veiled in an acronym I made up with my friends to describe our two least-favorite teachers. They'd earned this harsh nickname by making us do awful things, like being quiet in class and doing our homework. What horrible people!

B.B.I.H.

Tuesday
FEBRUARY 11

Today school went fine. But we made up something new - BBIH - that stands for BOth Bitches is here or ~~~~ Big Bitch is here. After school Ginger had voice lessons. Supper was pretty good.

P.S.= It's those things that make you go Hmmm. mmmmmm!!

— Dawn

Nothing closes an entry as controversial as this like some lyrics from C+C Music Factory ("hmm" being spelled with nine "m"s, of course).

Chapter 1

The word "butt" (or in my house, the B-word!) also occupied one of the top slots on our family's forbidden-curse-word list.

But that didn't stop me from writing it or, in this case, artfully depicting the anatomy in this incredibly lifelike image, logically captioned with an M.C. Hammer lyric.

Given my somewhat abstract artistic style, it's difficult to determine the identity of the suspect who's mooning. However, with hair like that, I suspect the guilty party might be none other than my megacrush, Bart Simpson.

Monday
MARCH 9

This morning I went to chorus. It was sorta fun. We went back to social studies today. BOOOOOOOOOOO!! My Lunch was exellent. After school we went ta get Tom's shot. We got a cookie!! For supper I had to wash.

P.S.= Can't touch this.

BOtt

Dawn

Also in this entry is the first of many references to my brother, Tom's, weekly allergy shots. I went along for the Highlights magazines in the waiting room and the inevitable cookie that followed.

Chapter 1

February 20, 1992, started out as a noteworthy day. I clearly got the better end of the deal in a lunchtime bartering ritual. As fifth-graders, we were like inmates, but, rather than cigarettes, our currency was Cool Ranch Doritos and Hi-C Ecto-Cooler. There was no greater score than unloading your boring pretzel sticks in exchange for Handi-Snacks or, better yet, a Kudos bar.

Feeling like hot stuff, with Ding Dongs coursing through my veins, I wrote my most controversial closing line thus far: an accidental reference to anal sex.

I was attempting to quote a lyric from the song "Da Butt" by Experience Unlimited. Note that the actual lyric of the song is "Doin' da butt" (a dance move). But, E.U., if you'd like the rights to this improved lyric, I'm sure we can work something out.

Thursday
FEBRUARY 20

Today we had Band. I'm becoming pretty good friends with Stephanie. At lunch she gave me half of her dia Dong fruit by the foot. After school I had dance. It was funer then usually for some reason. I watched Beverly Hills 90210 tonight and mom ate at the Gaylores man-chen tonight.

P.s.= Do it in the butt ALL NIGT LONG

Dawn

I can't recall the exact reason my mom was invited to dine with Nebraska royalty. She was probably accepting an award for introducing shoulder pads to the Midwest.

I'M TOO SEXY FOR MY . . . CAT SHIRT.

As an eleven-year-old model and trendsetter, with my finger on the pulse of fashion, I took exceptional care in getting dressed each morning. Because, seriously, how could the boys resist me in Guess jeans, a Limited Too sweatshirt, and a BeDazzled hat?

Here I sport my best Bridget-Fonda-from-Singles look.

Tonight we went on a magor shopping spree

today I got up and got dressed. I wore A swet shirt whith a cat on it. And I also wore jeans.

Apparently "TOO" stands for "too big."

Nothing masks a bad hair day like a heavily BeDazzled hat.

I wore my Red, White And blue dress, with Blue & white pants.

29

ESPRIT was one of my favorite brands. On a trip to Los Angeles, Ginger and I even got to visit the superstore. For such a special occasion, I simply had to wear my best fanny pack and knee-length stonewashed jean shorts.

> Today I wore my E-sprit outfit.

> I got new shoes today. They were white with Bright pink.

I got new Guess Jeans

Here I rock what I liked to call "recursive self-portrait overalls."

How many couches had to die for me to wear this outfit?

I wore one of my new outfits to school.

Chapter 1

Looking and acting older than you are is the ultimate mark of a cool preteen. I had this nailed. Sure, some of my friends might have passed for freshmen or sophomores, but I could pass for a senior . . . citizen.

I had a stamp collection *and* a coin collection. I watched *60 Minutes*. My favorite toy was my grandma's electric card-shuffler. I drank Ovaltine. I went mall walking.

This propensity for senior-citizen behavior is evidenced on January 9, 1991. I kept up my kid disguise throughout the school day, but as soon as the bell rang, I let my old-lady flag fly.

Jan. 9, 1991

Today I wore black pants, a white shirt, sweader, and socks & shoes. In my lunch I packed koo-laid, sandwich, krakers, and a Zinger. After school I went to the foot docter, I got cream for my Toe-nails. Then I went to the eye docters I got new lenses. Then I went to quier. Then Home.

Dawn

I ♥ CASEY KASEM

> March 29, 1992
> Top Ten Songs on KC's Top Forty
> ← 1st Row Artist   2nd Row → Songs
> ① Vanesa Williams
>   Save the Best for Last
> ② David E. Luis
>   Masterpeice
> ③ Micheal Jackon
>   Remember the time
> ④ Mariah Carey
>   Make it Happen
> ⑤
> ⑥
> ⑦ Color me Bad
>   Thinking bads
> ⑧ Micheal Bolton
>   Missing you now
> ⑨ Amy Grant
>   Good for me
> ⑩ ~~scribble~~ Cathy Catroolee
>   Everything Changes

I seem to have taken a Fruity Pebbles break during 5 and 6.

Aside from Sunday school and *Star Search*, my favorite Sunday-morning ritual was listening to the smooth voice of Casey Kasem counting down the Billboard hits on *American Top 40*.

I had important questions that only Casey could answer. Could Vanessa Williams hold the top spot for the fifth consecutive week? How far would Color Me Badd climb the charts? Had Mr. Big's "To Be With You" really been knocked out of the Top 10 already?! CASEY, TELL ME!

Chapter 2

PASSION ON THE PRAIRIE

Chapter 2

I decided that as a gorgeous, fashionable woman, I needed the perfect accessory: ~~a slap bracelet~~ a man.

I liked to think of myself as a preteen Casanova. I felt confident that boys would take one look at my thick bangs and permed bob and start swooning.

Yet somehow, no one was breaking down my door. Perhaps they were playing hard to get. Perhaps they couldn't handle a real woman. Perhaps they were intimidated by my *WWF* fandom. In any case, it was time for me to take matters into my own hands. After finding his address in the back of *Tiger Beat*, I wrote a letter to Kirk Cameron, granting him the honor of becoming my boyfriend. Sadly, my love letter must have gotten lost or something, because he never showed up at my house, despite my hand-drawn directions. "Turn right at the lopsided pine tree and left at the house with the red pickup."

If Kirk wasn't going to come through, I would have to make do with the upperclassmen of Humann Elementary.

March, 12, 1992
These are the boys I kinda like:

Tyler
Jason
Steve
Dan
Clint
Nolan
Ryan
Joe

I want to get busy with:
Jason, Clint, Nolan & Joe

Chapter 2

Luckily, there was one boy almost as cute as Kirk. That dreamboat was named Dan. Dan was the boy I most pined for in fifth grade and the subject of many diary entries. He had big brown eyes, was good at four square, and had a miniature schnauzer. What more could a visor-wearing, clarinet-playing girl ask for?

Who wouldn't have fallen for Dan's awesome fashion sense and dashing good looks? He was Lincoln's answer to Joey Lawrence. On this particular day, I had no choice but to make a move, one lifted from the *Edward Scissorhands* playbook.

April, 9, 1991

Today I thought Dan looked cuter then ever. He wore black shorts and a very big sweater. The other day Dan sat in front of me wile our teacher was reading. I slowly touched my hand to his genle back and scrached it softly. He looked back and smiled at me And I smiled at him. He IS A HUNK!!!

Dawn

It can be difficult to dress for Nebraska's unpredictable spring weather, but in his summer-on-the-bottom, winter-on-the-top ensemble, Dan was prepared for anything.

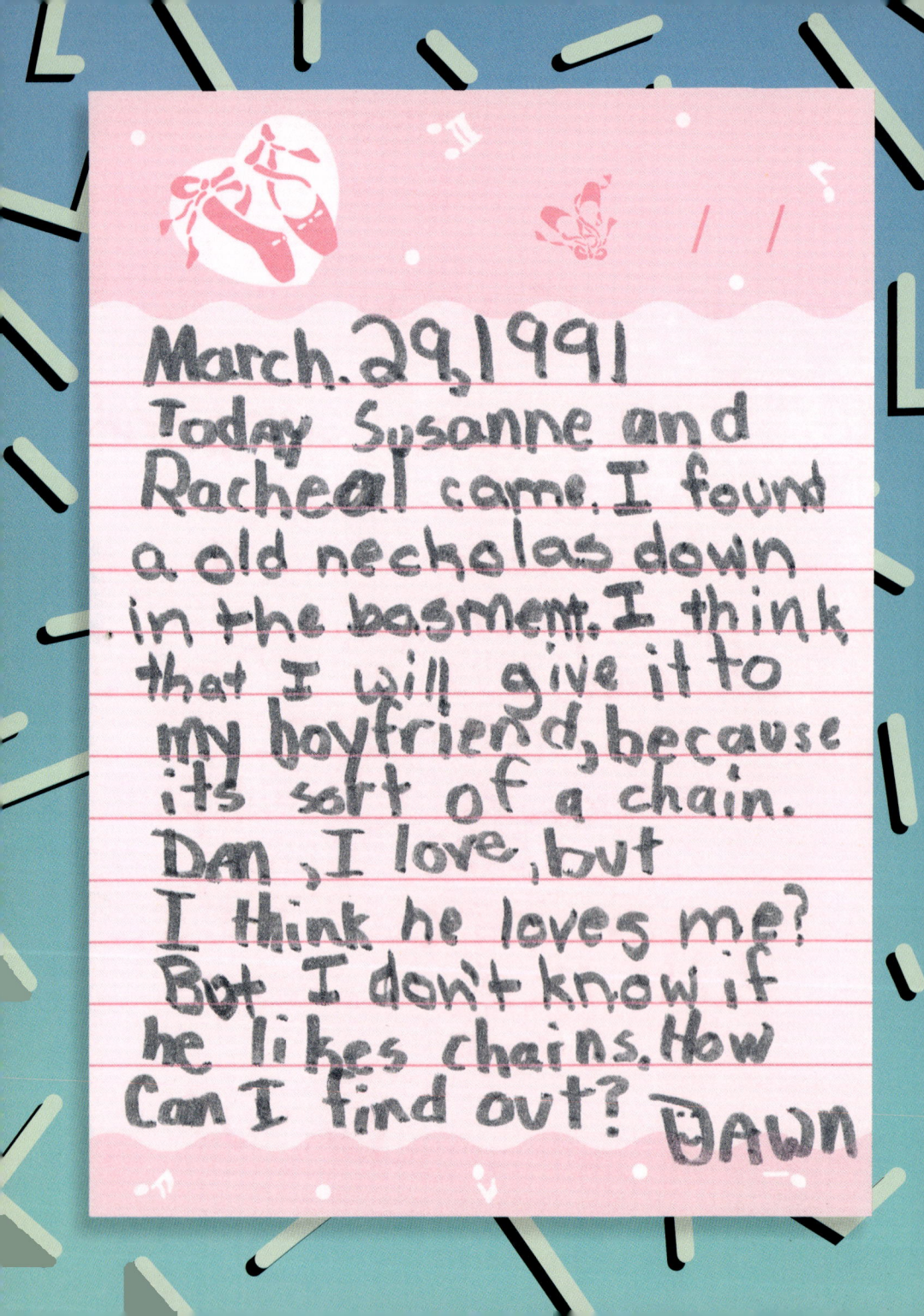

March 29, 1991
Today Susanne and Racheal came. I found a old necholas down in the basment. I think that I will give it to my boyfriend, because its sort of a chain. Dan, I love, but I think he loves me? But I don't know if he likes chains. How can I find out?

DAWN

I tried many things to show Dan that I loved him: I laughed at his jokes; I let him cut in front of me in the four square line; I scratched his back, for heaven's sake! The boy could not take a hint.

Drastic measures were called for, and what better way to express my feelings than with a gift? It was an ill-gotten gift, but it was a gift nonetheless.

And despite my reference to Dan as my boyfriend, I can say with absolute certainty that this was wishful thinking, unless you take "boyfriend" to mean "someone who occasionally sits in the same classroom as you because he is required to."

It's a Friday and Anne didn't invite me to her PARTY!

April 12, 1991

    Today we got to chose who we sat by in homeroom, but girls had to sit by boys & visaversa. Well, first of all maggie wanted to sit by Dan. But Dan wanted to sit by me and I wanted to sit by Dan so I did. And at reading I was behind aron trying to look at a book and Dan was siting by aron looking at it. And Dan said "let Dawn look". I LOVE DAN!

What better evidence of my love than a heart appearing in the "D" in Dan's name—every single time?

My moves were totally working. I knew if I continued refining my flirtation tactics, Dan and I would soon be the Zack and Kelly of Humann Elementary, sharing a milkshake at The Max, or our version of The Max: Arby's of South Lincoln.

On April 12, 1991, I learned that Dan was more than just a pretty face. He was a man of honor, and he proved it to me in the noblest way he knew how: asking Aron to let me find Waldo. Looking back, I only feel bad that our love was thrown in Maggie's face in such a blatant display of Dan's chivalry. Just kidding. IT FELT AMAZING.

However, prevailing over Maggie proved to have unforeseen consequences. I did not get invited to Anne's slumber party, where I undoubtedly missed the opportunity to have my training bra frozen.

Chapter 2

I liked Dan for many reasons. He wasn't just noble. He was also a rebel. That independent spirit came out in full force on the last day of school.

And his defiant behavior was contagious. Inspired by Dan's act of rebellion, I used this opportunity to mouth off to my mom (in secret, written form).

But I was just getting started. I then wrote the ultimate forbidden word: "sex." And I repeated it ten times just to make myself clear.

I must confess, I didn't know much about the subject, so I felt compelled to turn to my role models, Salt-N-Pepa. From their music video for "Let's Talk About Sex," I learned that sex involved dancing in overalls and color-blocked mock turtlenecks. No wonder my interest was piqued.

May 26, 1991
School got out 2 day ago! Dan held up a big banner that said WERE FREE. I like his style. I'm gonna miss him. my mom's acting like a jerk latly. I love the word sex so sex sex sex sex sex sex sex sex, get the point. SEX!
— Dawn

My mom probably earned the "jerk" label because she asked me to do something unthinkable, like unload the dishwasher.

Chapter 2

Because Dan lived in another neighborhood, the end of the school year meant the beginning of a long-distance relationship, one that our love was not strong enough to overcome.

A lot can happen in a summer, and this summer was especially illuminating. My worldview changed forever. I saw *Bill & Ted's Bogus Journey*. I tried Fruit Stripe gum. I got to level 100 in Bubble Bobble. I visited Omaha.

Just as the seasons change and permed hair becomes straight and Girbaud jeans replace Z. Cavariccis, a series of eligible bachelors took Dan's place in my heart.

First on my list of conquests was Nolan. Nolan had white-blond hair and porcelain skin. Incredibly smart, he was pretty much the *Little Man Tate* of our class. His ability to explain to me the difference between the Senate and the House of Representatives melted my heart.

Monday
SEPTEMBER 14

Today we went back to school. We had social studies. We studied maps and stuff. After school I went to the park. I hugged Nolan. He's wierd.

P.S. = SLEEP!!

DAWN

Can we all agree that a more appropriate name for Social Studies is "Maps and Stuff"?

Chapter 2

My subtle methods of flirtation weren't working. Wearing my brightest Hypercolor T-shirt and throwing around gold chains had failed to ensnare Dan *or* Nolan. It was time to cast a wider net.

But juggling all this man candy can be difficult and I found it increasingly necessary to keep tabs on my progress with each of them. Any sophisticated woman knows of the many ways to tell if a guy likes you, and, indeed, Aaron's simply *seeing* me—no doubt in Umbros and a banana clip—was proof of his affection.

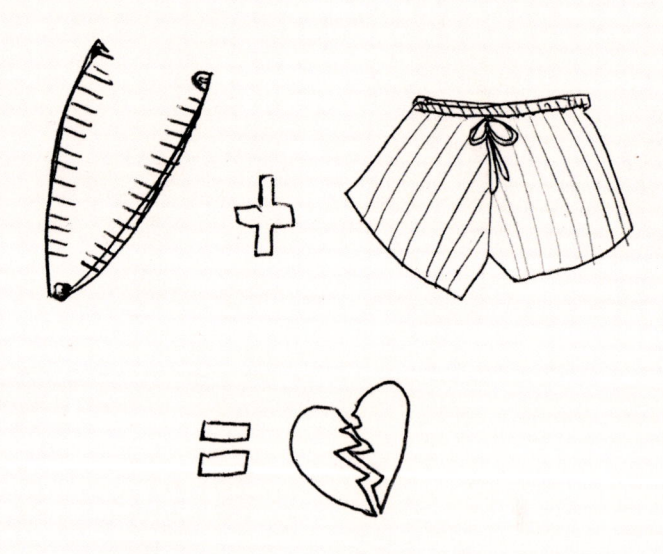

Tuesday
APRIL 7

Today was alright. I like Steve ~~okay~~ Aaron ~~scratched~~ Clint ~~okay~~. Steve talked with me, Aaron saw me, And Clint talked to me alone after school. After school Ginger's voice got cancel 4 hour- We had 4-H tonight.

P.S.=Caromolo

Dawn

Throughout my diaries, I felt compelled to track the schedule of my sister. Ginger was a regular songbird with a vast catalog of Bette Midler covers. How could the cancellation of her voice lesson not be top news?

Chapter 2

Valentine's Day was *the* event of the season. Crushes were revealed, hearts were broken, and on the *90210* Valentine's Day special, Dylan took Brenda to donate blood. It was *huge*.

Because a holiday celebrating adult romantic love is totally appropriate for prepubescents, our school threw a party that included an exchange of valentines. Nothing says "I love you" like a *Garfield*-themed piece of cardboard.

Reading these valentines was always fifteen minutes of excitement and terror as you desperately hunted for subtle clues to uncover who might like you. If Nolan's *Teenage Mutant Ninja Turtles* valentine said "You have a pizza my heart," you knew he wanted to be your boyfriend. On the downside, if Aaron's Michael Jordan valentine said "No one could fill your shoes," you had to accept that his feelings were platonic, and his *seeing* you did not, in fact, mean what you thought.

But of all the valentines I received, it was my neighbor Clint who ended up blowing me away by unveiling his eternal devotion. Clint was a thoughtful, quiet boy with glasses almost as thick as mine. He was kind of a big deal on our block. Not only did he have a color computer, he also had a Super Soaker 200.

Tragically, our burgeoning love affair was cut short by my meddling friend Renee and things spiraled out of control. Stuff got so real, it drove me to write down one of my first curse words.

Feb. 14, 1992
Today is Valentines day we didn't have school. Yesterday we had our Valentines party. Clint (our next door neighbor) gave me a Valentine and on the back it said TO DAWN, I LOVE YOU. Love Clint. I told Reehe and she went overe

to clint and said "Dawn wonders if you want to go out w/ her" I never said that. Now I don't know what in the H, E, double, hocky-stick is going on.

Dawn

Chapter 2

With so many men in my life, I needed to figure out who my one true love was. Not sure where to turn, I decided to consult a supernatural power.

My opportunity arrived at my friend Jamie's slumber party, where she introduced me to something even more powerful than the Magic 8 Ball: the Ouija (or "weegee") board. Jamie didn't waste her time playing Mall Madness or Girl Talk like the rest of us rubes. She was into some serious black magic.

In Jamie's pink Wiccan chamber we used the power of the Ouija board to contact every last dead person we could think of: Lisa's grandma; my cat, April; and Marilyn Monroe.

Eventually we ran out of souls, so we moved on to finding out who our true loves were—something that is definitely known and oft discussed by the spirits. What else do they have going on? The magic Ouija board (and not my fingers, thank you very much) confirmed my admirer once and for all.

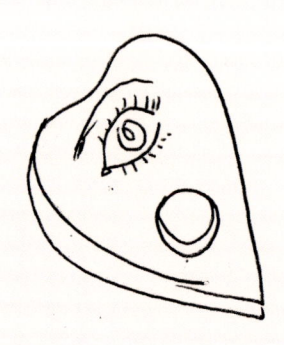

Tuesday
MARCH 24

Today I almost got homework in math, but, I finished. Lunch was very good. After school I found out mom got a job at a traveling agency. Ginger had voice lessons. Tonight we did weegee board.

P.S. = It said "Clint ♥'s Dawn.

Dawn

Observe, again, my fixation on Ginger's schedule. What was I, her secretary?

Chapter 2

Despite Clint's profession of love and the Ouija board's confirmation of our eternal connection, cruel fate soon reared its ugly head. Clint moved away—far from Nebraska to a more exotic locale: Wisconsin. (Um, where was the Ouija board on *that* piece of information?!)

With the end of an epic love affair often comes a rebound relationship, and in seventh grade I "went out" with a boy named Jack for about a month. Jack was a man of few words but easy on the eyes—a young Luke Perry with Airwalks and a JanSport backpack. Our courtship consisted of sitting next to each other on the bus in silence to and from school and one date where we rode our bikes to Walgreens and looked at magnets (second base).

However, our mutual interest in refrigerator decoration could not keep us together, and Jack broke up with me by telling Kyle to tell Renee to tell me it was over (I thought magnets stuck together!). Forget lawyers—in junior high it only takes a game of telephone to get a divorce.

Apparently cursed by the spirit world, I would be well into college before I had my next boyfriend. But in the meantime, at least I had my cat.

55

90210.M.G.

There was one television show I watched more devoutly than any other—*Beverly Hills, 90210*. This landmark program truly showed me the kind of teenager I wanted to grow into: a sophisticated Californian with Kelly's sleek blond hair, Dylan's rebellious nature, and Donna's quirky sense of style.

But I suspect that my parents did not think *90210* was appropriate for me. In a house where the phrase "that sucks" was off-limits, I knew I was not to be watching Brandon drunk drive, Steve try steroids, or Brenda take a pregnancy test. So every Thursday night, under the cover of darkness (my Op hoodie), I would sneak into our den and watch the scandal unfold on low volume with my face inches from the television.

After the show I'd carefully note a review of the week's episode. To provide some insight on these reviews, I've included a summary of what actually aired on that date.

P.S. = 90210 was not tonight.

Dylan visits his father in jail.

The Peach Pit is robbed and Brenda confronts the thief.

P.S. = 90210 was groosome tonight!!

> P.S. = 90210 was awsome tonight.

Brandon dates Trish, an Olympic figure skater.

Kelly hits it off with a man building her mother's wedding canopy.

> P.S. = 90210 was cute tonight!!

> P.S. = 90210 was dynamic tonight.

Brandon goes undercover for The West Beverly Blaze to expose the school's steroid problem.

Color Me Badd makes a guest appearance.

> P.S. = 90210 was stimulating tonight!!

> P.S.S. = 90210 was sexy tonight!

Andrea heads up an initiative to introduce condoms into the school.

> P.S. = 90210 was groovy tonight!!

Andrea goes to the horse racing track with Nat.

57

Chapter 3

REMEMBERING THE '90s

The early '90s were a time of extraordinary events and unforgettable icons on par with the Renaissance or Industrial Revolution. After all, what other era can claim Koosh balls *and* Reebok Pumps among its inventions?

It was an influential time in every medium. This groundbreaking period birthed such musical legends as P.M. Dawn, the Crash Test Dummies, and not one but two long-haired music duos: Milli Vanilli and Nelson. It was also a landmark time for toys—Skip-It, troll dolls, and Gak spread like wildfire through Humann Elementary. But most important, it was the golden age of television.

As a kid, I spent a *lot* of time watching television. From the Fox prime-time lineup, ABC's TGIF block, and Nickelodeon I learned all of life's important lessons, like:

1. How to dance with a sprained ankle. (*Saved by the Bell*)
2. Cool people have a best friend whose name is a number. (*Blossom*)
3. It's completely normal to find yourself on stage with the Beach Boys. Twice. (*Full House*)
4. A school board will overlook your suspension and allow you to graduate if your friends stage a walkout. (*Beverly Hills, 90210*)
5. Sometimes your best friend can turn into a porcelain doll. (*Are You Afraid of the Dark?*)

Who would I be without these lessons? Probably someone who reads books.

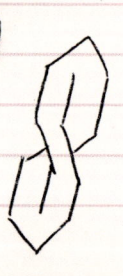

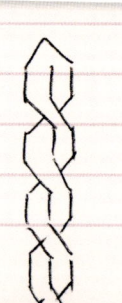

Chapter 3

TROLLING

In the span of three months, August through October of 1992, I bring up one particular topic a total of eleven times. Forget about Dan and Clint and *90210*; I had a new obsession—trolls. I had become fully crazed for these tiny plastic dolls with their brightly colored, untamed hair. I couldn't collect them fast enough. Sure, I already had a cat troll, clown troll, snorkeling troll, baby troll, Rollerblade troll, Halloween troll earrings, and the entire troll wedding party, but I needed more. I would not be satisfied until I had them all—or at least until 1993, when I discovered Pogs.

Ginger gave me a cat troll.

I got a troll.

Date Jan. 21, 1996, Sunday.

Today we din'nt go to sunday school and church. We din'nt go because dad had some work to do. We watched T.V. First we watched a show called Wild and Crazie kids. Then we watched a show called sk8 T.V. For lunch we had lasgne. After lunch I watched more T.V. It was kind of fun. For supper we had cheseburgers and chip's. Then I watched a show called America's Funniest home video's

Ever the refined lady, I spent this leisurely Sunday enjoying the finer things in life: cheeseburgers and Nickelodeon. I'm certain Jesus understood how important it was for me to miss Sunday school in order to put in a good eight hours in front of the boob tube. After all, Sunday is a day of rest!

The remarkable programs noted in this entry were all early-'90s classics. On the nearly impossible chance you've forgotten them, the following is a brief recap.

Wild & Crazy Kids pitted three teams of preteens in oversize, primary-colored T-shirts against one another in such intellectually stimulating events as Human Battleship and Donkey Basketball. These usually incorporated pies or slime.

SK8-TV followed skateboarders as they kickflipped and ollied their way through the most treacherous skate parks in America. As previously mentioned, skateboarders were at the top of my crush list. I dreamed of riding on the back of Tony Hawk's longboard down the Venice Beach boardwalk, one hand clinging tightly to his torso, the other holding a DQ Mr. Misty.

America's Funniest Home Videos elevated television to a work of art, with clips of kids saying inappropriate things, pets falling off swing sets, and dads taking softballs to the groin. Plus, any show that featured Bob Saget had my faithful viewership.

Chapter 3

Certain television shows embody an era. The '50s had *I Love Lucy*. The '60s had *Bewitched*. The '70s had *All in the Family*. The '80s were all about *Family Ties*. The early '90s: *The Heights*.

This hallmark of television brilliance (tragically canceled after one season) followed a ragtag rock band with a steamy front man played by Jamie Walters. Like many lead singers, he was a motorcycle-riding mechanic by day and a singer/songwriter by night.

The theme song (memorialized in my postscript) went on to top the Billboard charts, thanks in large part to one of the best saxophone solos ever recorded.

Jamie's raspy voice made me forget about my boring day and growling stomach.

Thursday
OCTOBER 1

Today I was office helper. It was quite borring. I skipped lunch. After school I went to dance. It was so fun. Ginger had play practice. I watched "The Heights"!!

P.S.= How do you talk to an angel?

— Dawn

> OK, here's a fun game: from now on, you take a drink every time I talk about Ginger's schedule.

WWF MANIA

> P.S.= WWF was on!!

In the early '90s, I was completely infatuated with professional wrestling. Nothing got my heart pumping like seeing the steamy (and worldly) British Bulldog hit Jake "The Snake" Roberts over the head with a folding chair. And when the terrifying Undertaker locked The Ultimate Warrior in an airtight casket, I had nightmares for weeks.

I think historians can agree that the greatest tragedy of the twentieth century was when my parents refused to let me order *SummerSlam* on pay-per-view.

> P.S.= There was a 2 hour special of WWF wrestling tonight.

> There was a 40 men match on WWF prime time. It was the first ever.

And what kind of fan would I be without a Hulk Hogan plush?

67

Chapter 3

As a sophisticated viewer, I could not survive solely on rock-star man candy and buckets of slime being dumped on people's heads. To satisfy my more mature tastes, there was *thirtysomething*.

This drama followed the lives of married couple Michael and Hope and their group of friends, who, as you might have deduced, were all in their thirties. Though my biggest hardships at eleven were Dan's not yet professing his undying love and the injustice of occasionally having to change the kitty litter, I could still sympathize with the stress Michael and Hope endured as new parents, as well as the strain in Nancy and Elliot's marriage thanks to Elliot's infidelity. These sorts of issues were commonplace at Humann Elementary.

**Tuesday
MARCH 3**

Today my lunch was very good. Today is teacher's appriciation day, the school was decorated. After school Ginger had voice lessons. Tonight we had a 4-H meeting at our house. It was fun. we made fruit pizzas. 4-H is always fun!!

P.S.= Mom's favorite show (Thirtysomething) came back on T.V.!

Dawn

Ahem—*Ginger* had voice lessons. Did you take a drink?

Chapter 3

When I managed to tear myself away from the television, I occasionally entertained myself by reading. My go-to series was The Baby-sitters Club. I dreamed of hanging out with the girls in Stony Brook, Connecticut. I'd spend my afternoons making funky jewelry with Claudia and being bossed around by Kristy. I wanted to be just like sophisticated Stacey (minus the diabetes).

But what I really couldn't put down was *Where's Waldo?* Sure, they were books without words, but they were literary classics. Waldo was so cute, with his little cane and glasses. I couldn't help but be jealous of his girlfriend, Wenda.

I was so into Waldo that I handed out *Where's Waldo?* valentines to my whole class in 1992. After all, what better courier of affection than a skinny, middle-aged, bespectacled man with a striped turtleneck hiding out in a crowd? Although, on a 2" x 3" card, Waldo was, admittedly, pretty easy to find.

Monday
FEBRUARY 10

This morning I went to chorus. It was sorta fun. School was normal. Lunch was o.k. After school we went to get Tom's shot. We also got Valentines. Me & Ginger got Where's Waldo wathes. Tonight we went to the school skate.

P.S.= We had ham for supper

Dawn

Looks like Tom's shot bumped ham to the postscript.

Chapter 3

No place encapsulates the early '90s like the mall. In Lincoln, our shoppers' paradise was called Gateway.

With so many amazing places to spend my hard-earned allowance, I could while away hour after hour in this preteen dreamland. On January 16, 1992, I shopped till I dropped at only the most high-end stores Gateway had to offer:

Thingsville, with its one-stop shopping for trolls, drip candles, and rainsticks, was the ultimate destination for birthday-party presents.

B. Dalton was the hippest bookstore and perfect place to get your hands on the latest Lurlene McDaniel tale of teenage mortality or the hottest new read, *The Face on the Milk Carton*. (Is it wrong that I was jealous of that kidnapped girl?)

Claire's was the coolest accessory franchise and the only place to get your yin-yang choker, best-friend locket, and peace-sign earrings.

The Incredible Bulk, a bi-level candy store, is, coincidentally, where I spent the incredible bulk of my allowance. With my insatiable sweet tooth, I found this candy palace irresistible. From its Tear Jerkers to Bubble Tape to baseball-sized jawbreakers, The Incredible Bulk was directly responsible for maintaining my four-cavities-a-year standard.

Thursday, JANUARY 16

Today I started my 1st day off by going to Gateway with Ginger and mom. Me & Ginger went to the Incredible Bulk. We got about 50 mini year jerkers, sour apple, grape, & cherry chewable candies, and Sour Balls. We also went to B. dalton, thingsville, Claires jewarie, the original cookie and other clothing stores. AT noon we we went to the YMCA to workout. I lost 2½ pounds. After that we went to dance I saw my recidal costume, IT's so cool. Then we ate supper!

P.S.= We had walfuls for supper!

Dawn

I may have worked out at the YMCA this day, but I suspect my weight loss had more to do with malnutrition than exercise.

Chapter 3

Having an array of cool writing utensils was essential for any self-respecting early-'90s preteen. Atop the pen hierarchy were Lisa Frank and Sanrio, whose pens were decorated with unicorns or Keroppi the frog. If animals weren't your thing, there were pens with scented ink or interchangeable tips so you could switch from blue to purple to pink in seconds. If you decided to go the pencil route, Yikes! triangular pencils were the best, and they provided the perfect perch for the requisite troll pencil-topper.

Just when I thought my pen collection couldn't get any cooler, along came an ink-filled wonder that changed everything: the Squiggle Wiggle Writer. The ultimate in writing technology, this battery-powered marvel spun in tiny circles, creating the most magnificent handwriting known to man. Though this miracle elevated my previous scribbles to calligraphic masterpieces, the pen's unwieldiness took a toll, as noted in the postscript.

Monday
JANUARY 27

Today was o.k. at school, but we had a substitute in Math, Reading, and P.E. Lunch was good! After school Ginger had spanish. I mostly watched T.V. Tonight there was a Nebraska game. They lost.

P.S.= Now my hand feels weird.

Dawn

> *Also, if you're still playing the Ginger's-schedule drinking game, congratulations! You're now an alcoholic.*

Chapter 3

There are a number of early-'90s catchphrases that have, sadly, fallen out of fashion. Such zingers as "Don't have a cow" and "Take a chill pill" sit in the lexical dustbin atop their '80s cousins "Totally!" and "Gag me with a spoon."

Surprisingly, "Eat my shorts" has stood the test of time, and I used it this morning.

But one '90s phrase, a single word in particular, was more clever and powerful than them all. That word was "Not!"

"Not!" was awesome, because it automatically got you out of anything you said. If you opened your mouth about something, only to receive puzzled looks from your peers ("*Encino Man* was based on a true story, right?"), you only had to follow it up with a quick "Not!", and you were completely off the hook.

On April 1, 1992, I made good use of it to reverse my dramatic, albeit poetic, reaction to my mom's cruelly abandoning her family to start a part-time job at a travel agency. She *should* have been sitting at home all day, missing her beautiful and dynamic daughter. How dare she have a life?!

However, the day after writing this angst-filled entry, I must have felt a little guilty. By scrawling a gigantic "NOT!" across my angry words, it was like they'd never existed.

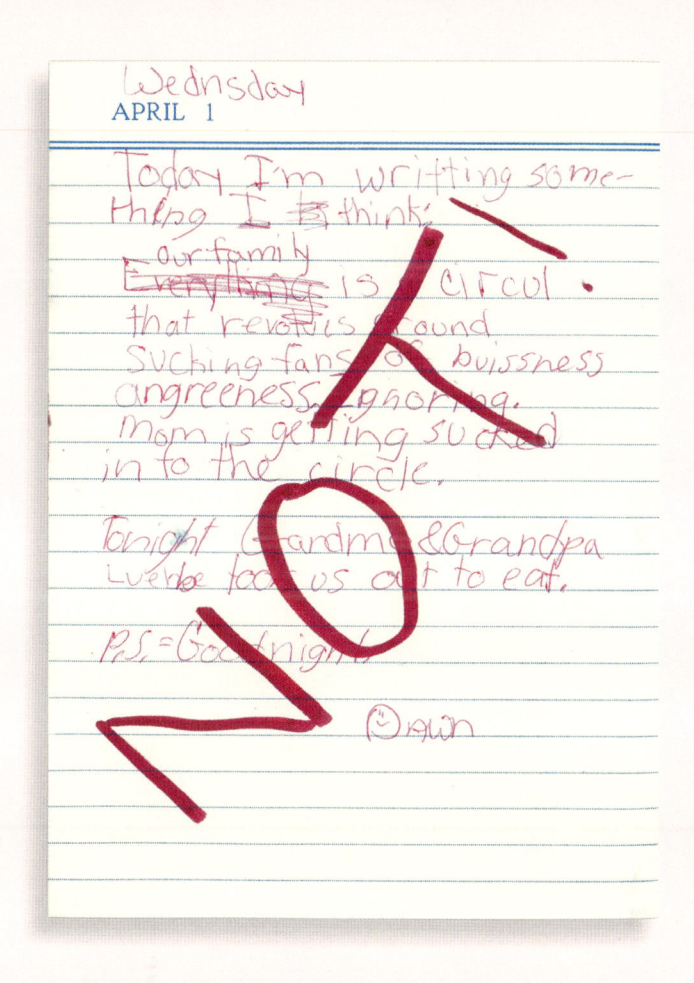

As the giant "NOT!" makes this entry rather difficult to decipher, I have transcribed it for easier reading:

"Today I'm writing something I think: Our family is a circle that revolves around sucking fans of business angriness. Ignoring. Mom is getting sucked into that circle. Tonight Grandma and Grandpa Luebbe took us out to eat.
P.S. Good night."

Even in my anger, supper still warrants a mention.

77

Chapter 4

UNTALENTED:

A Collection of Failed Hobbies

As I mentioned previously (in almost every single entry), most of my free time as a preteen was dedicated to the great American pastimes of eating junk food and watching television. But even the most devoted *Full House* scholar must broaden her horizons, so I pursued a number of hobbies.

Sports were out of the question, mostly from lack of interest but also due to a complete absence of natural athletic ability. But never one to pooh-pooh something without trying it (unless that thing was a vegetable), I tried my hand at sports. Twice.

My first foray into "sports" was playing Duck Hunt on my brother's Nintendo. But despite my best efforts, I could never hit those darn ducks, and I'd get seriously miffed when that dumb dog laughed at me.

My second and final attempt left me with a head wound sustained during a game of miniature golf. I made the rookie mistake of standing behind my Arnold Palmer–esque sister while she tried for the free-game hole.

No more sports for me, thank you very much. It was time to consider other, slightly less dangerous activities.

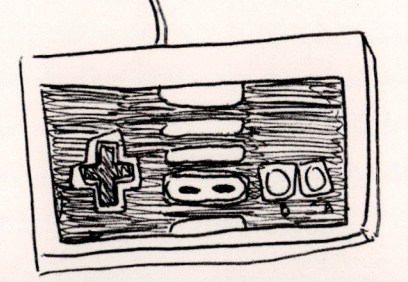

Chapter 4

Ever the vision of beauty and grace, my favorite hobby was dance. But I didn't waste my time with the more classical (er, respectable) forms like ballet and tap. I only had eyes for jazz. Jazz hands were my ticket to becoming the next member of the Fly Girls on *In Living Color*.

Who cares that I was, hands down, the worst dancer in my class year after year? Who cares that I had no knack for memorizing choreography? Who cares that my lack of coordination prevented me from doing 90 percent of the dance steps? I would not let anything stop me from becoming a hip-hop master.

On January 11, 1990, I call attention to our yearly dance recital. It was a much-anticipated event and the culmination of countless hours of hitch-kicking and cabbage-patching. We practiced for months in preparation for our performance at Pershing Auditorium, Lincoln's answer to Carnegie Hall. Performing at Pershing was my ticket out of Dodge. Surely the majority of industry professionals did their talent scouting in Lincoln.

Date Jan. 11, 1990, ~~We~~ Thursday

Today for breakfast I had a muffin. I also had orange juise. At reading we had a test. At math we got to eat an orange. I was fun. For lunch I had a chicken paddie and French Fri's and milk. After school I went to dance. We found out what our recidle song. It was going to be pink cadulack. That was one of my favoite songs. for supper we had spegetti. It was very good. Dawn

And, like a marathon runner, any serious jazz dancer must carbo-load before a big event.

Chapter 4

One of the most exciting parts of the dance recital was the costumes. Composed of an endless array of sequined halter tops, knee pads, catsuits, and hair scrunchies, my look was poised to take its place in pop-icon fashion history alongside Madonna's cone bra and M.C. Hammer's harem pants. Feast your eyes on my radiant "Pink Cadillac" recital costume:

Was I the new poster child for scoliosis awareness?

Here, the addition of a tie allowed me to go straight from dance recital to the office.

83

Chapter 4

I'm sure the mesh over the midsection was definitely supposed to be that baggy (or was possibly a last-minute alteration in response to my abnormally long torso).

Note the amazing attention to detail.

See how the shape of my skirt matches my perm?

And I guess our recital song that year must have been "I'm a Little Teapot," or possibly the lesser-known hit, "You must be this tall to ride this ride."

Chapter 4

Of course, dance was just one of my many awe-inspiring talents. At age ten, with music on my mind, I had my pick of instruments. I could have gone the predictable route and chosen the instrument favored by the popular girls, the flute. Or I could have channeled my inner badass and picked the saxophone or drums. But why waste my time on any of those, when I could toot the sexiest of all instruments, the most sensual of woodwinds—the clarinet?

Since my hip-hop dancing career hadn't quite taken off, I figured music was my next best shot at fame. After all, when you look at photos of '90s pop groups, the one thing they all seemed to be missing was a skinny clarinetist.

But I knew stardom wouldn't come without practice, so every day I devoutly tightened my ligature and let waves of melodic perfection wash over me, all the while picturing myself as the fourth member of TLC.

Most of our repertoire was boring classical stuff, but occasionally we'd get to play a pop song. It was only a matter of time before I'd hit the road with T-Boz, Left Eye, and Chilli. All I had to do was decide on my stage name—would it be Both Eyes or 2Tall?

On January 23, 1992, we covered a pop classic by the Beach Boys. Who better to celebrate surfing than a bunch of landlocked preteens?

Thursday!
JANUARY 23

This morning I went to band. We started practicing Surfin U.S.A. We sounded OK :) I had a good lunch. After school dad went to parnet/teacher conferences for the first time. Mom went to parent visitation at my dance. We went home to eat we had vegie soup. I wached 90210 (of corse), mom had a meeting, and Ginger had Gymnastics.

P.S.= Tom get the heck of my diary.

Dawn

> *I'm not really sure which part of this scandalous entry I was so scared of my brother, Tom, reading—the part about parent-teacher conferences or the part about soup.*

Chapter 4

Rockin' around the Christmas tree.

GROOVE IS IN THE ~~HEART~~ POSTSCRIPT.

Never quite able to grasp the correct use of a postscript, I spent many weeks using popular song lyrics to express my closing thoughts.

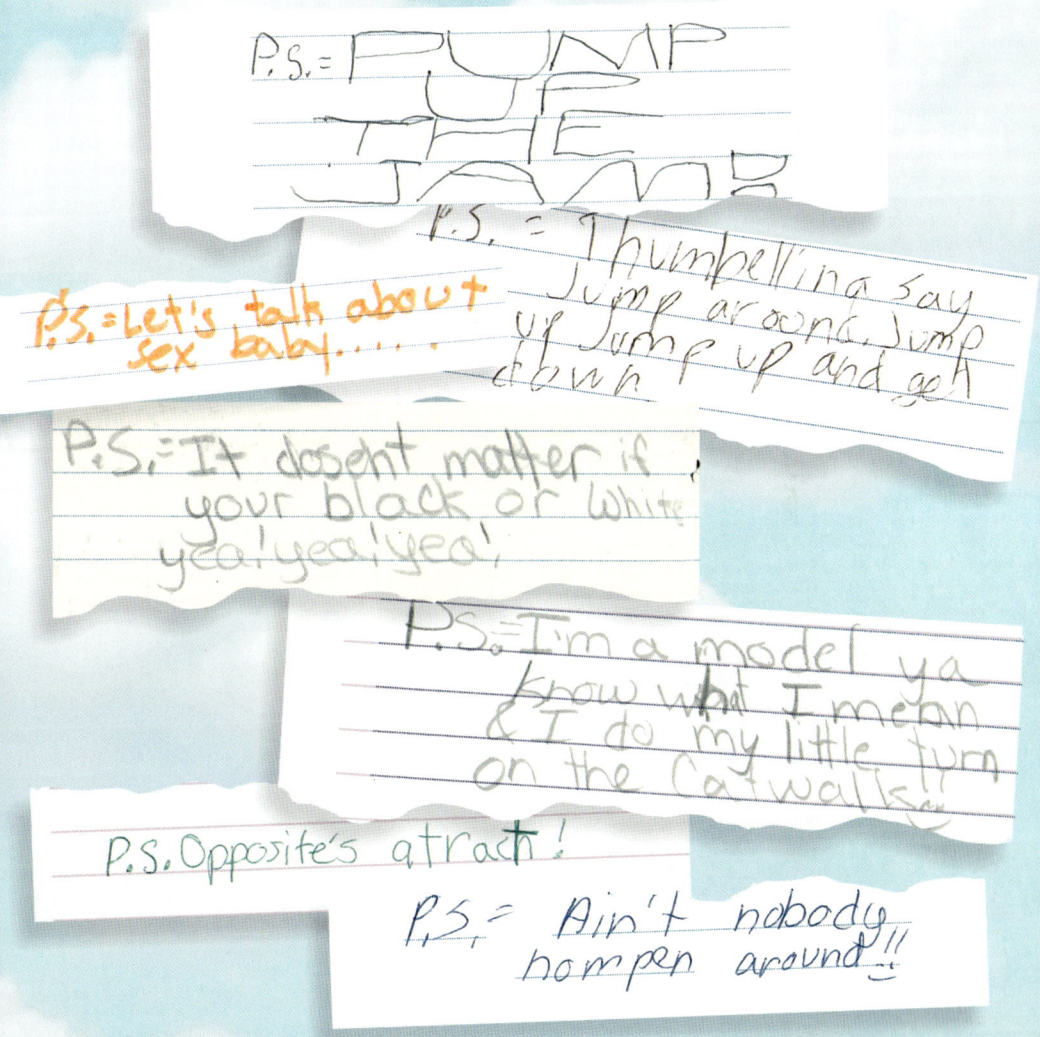

P.S.= PUMP UP THE JAM

P.S.=Let's talk about sex baby....

P.S.= Thumbelling say Jump around, Jump up Jump up and get down

P.S.= It dosent matter if your black or white yea! yea! yea!

P.S.= I'm a model ya know what I mean & I do my little turn on the catwalk

P.S. Opposite's atract!

P.S.= Ain't nobody hompen around!!

Chapter 4

I know what you're all wondering right now. "But, Dawn, when did you enroll in modeling school?" Well, I'll tell you. It was the summer of 1992. Not everyone is born with beauty, style, *and* grace. Some of us have to go to modeling school, namely, the Nancy Bounds Modeling School of Lincoln.

Under Nancy Bounds's expert tutelage, we took classes in makeup, choosing a wardrobe, walking the runway, and, most important, manners. We all know that Tyra Banks got to where she is by throwing around a lot of Please's and Thank You's.

We also learned that any successful model must watch what she eats. Kate Moss once said, "Nothing tastes as good as skinny feels." Clearly, she had never tried Nibs.

Tuesday
JULY 7

Today I ran some errans with dad, Ginger had acting Academy again today. For lunch I made a turkey sandwich. Today I rode up to Hy-vee by my-self. I got Nibs, a Doctor Pepper, and Melon Heads. I went with dad to pick up Ginger I got a Pepsi there. Tonight I went to Modeling rehersal for fasian Walk. I walked on the run way about 50 times. they bought us pop from Davingi's.

P.S.= I had 3 pops today!!

*Forget heroin-chic.
With my three-pops-a-day
habit, I was Dr Pepper–chic.*

Chapter __4__

To celebrate graduation from modeling school, we performed a fashion show for an audience of ~~Vogue columnists, fashion designers, and celebrities~~ proud parents. When I sashayed down the catwalk to Billy Ray Cyrus, I'm pretty sure I was mistaken for Cindy Crawford. She had recently wowed at Paris Fashion Week in her own Disney-themed denim vest with matching high-waisted shorts, three pairs of layered socks, and turquoise hair scrunchie.

I'm no body language expert, but I'm pretty sure that all those audience members resting their heads on their hands were showing signs of intense interest.

My day may have started off with chores and allergy shots, but my night was filled with fashion, finesse, and flowers.

92

Tuesday JULY 21

This morning mom went to work early, me and Ginger emptyed dishwaster and reloaded. It was very very boring until about 5:00 pm. We took tom to get his shot, and a cookie, then we dropped tom off at a team barbaque. Then mom dropped me off at modeling. Tonight we preformed a cic breakie heart, I got a rose. Mom and Ginger watched. Tonight Dad helped with my stamp collection.

P.S.= Hi, I Tommie the tomato head. → ☺

Dawn

After a long day of modeling, Cindy also probably went home and worked on her stamp collection.

DAWN LUEBBE PLATH, PRETEEN POET

Clearly an excellent writer, I eventually decided to kick things up a notch and try my hand at poetry.

The following poems appear at the back of my 1992 diary but were actually written in 1994. I was thirteen by then and had found a more mature voice.

Rather than take my inspiration from happy things such as love and nature, I stuck to dark topics like fear and death. I had seen *Are You Afraid of the Dark?* and read R. L. Stine, and I knew what fear truly was.

> **OCTOBER 11**
> Today is really June 6 1994
>
> Fear
>
> Run
> but where to
> Hide
> but from what
> Cry
> but what will it do
> Scream
> but who shall hear
> Die
> but why betray life

The following poem was inked after Kurt Loder interrupted *The Real World: San Francisco* to break the news of Kurt Cobain's passing.

OCTOBER 12

Feeling free. Be the wind
Blow light. Blow fearce,
First a sutter concouraging
win than strong. Then
slowely die.

Do

Kirk Kobane

Chapter 5

PRETEEN CONFLICT:

The Art of Overreaction

I was lucky to have a happy and carefree childhood. The biggest tragedy of my early years was probably the time I dropped my Walkman into the toilet. Perhaps in an effort to add a little drama to my life, certain minor conflicts with family and friends were blown out of proportion.

Always one to avoid confrontation at all costs, I'd rarely get into fights. Instead, I'd keep my feelings bottled up and enjoy some good old-fashioned inner turmoil. At home, most of my annoyance was reserved for my brother, Tom, but on rare occasions my sister, Ginger, could push my buttons, too. I'd also get miffed when my parents failed to sufficiently compliment me on a rockin' clarinet solo. And one day I remember feeling overly concerned when Renee didn't sit next to me at lunch. (Was it because I wore the same pair of Guess jeans as her?!)

While my fear of confrontation stopped me from properly resolving these issues in person, it didn't stop me from expressing my angst on paper through a potent combination of exaggerations and misspellings.

Jan, 3, 1991.

Today I wore a blue outfit with pink lace and blue hearts on it. For lunch I packed string cheese, sandwich, Chips, and choc. milk. After school I went home and got into my dance outfit and when we got there it was closed & mom YELLED AT ME Then mom said "You'll have to go to gate way with us." I said "ok" Then mom yelled at me And said "I'm takeing you home" And I said "ok" And mom YELLED AT ME the rest of the way home!

Dawn

January 3, 1991, started out great. Sure, my wardrobe choice was more suitable for a toddler than a tween, but no doubt I rocked it as I sashayed past Dan in homeroom.

Making a lunchtime appearance that day was that wonder of culinary science, string cheese, which had recently made its debut at Humann Elementary. It was all the rage, because everyone knows that cheese is so much tastier in thread form.

After school, I headed to dance class, ready to pivot-turn and butterfly my way through "Pump Up the Jam." Seriously, the only thing that could have made the day better was a new episode of *Just the Ten of Us*.

But then—just like that—everything fell apart. Dance class was canceled, and my mom turned into a monster. Not only did she yell at me (which involved calmly expressing annoyance at my failure to remind her that dance was canceled), but she also threatened to take me to Gateway (the mall). How dare she?!

It was days like this I seriously considered running away to New York City to find the family from *My Two Dads*. Nicole Bradford didn't know how good she had it.

Chapter 5

As if dealing with an unreasonable mother wasn't enough, I also had my annoying older brother to contend with.

Having a big brother is great as an adult, but as a kid it sucks. (I mean, stinks! Sorry, Mom!) The only time he came in handy was when I was a dollar short for my Scholastic book club order and I'd raid his money tin—Bo Jackson pencil case—for quarters. I'd let nothing stand in the way of having the latest Babysitters Club Super Special and cat stickers.

From his "I know you are, but what am I?" to the rubber bands he shot at me, practically everything Tom did bugged the heck out of me. Just look at this punk:

You can see why one of my biggest worries was Tom's getting his hands on my diary, that sacred place where I expressed my most private thoughts and feelings—like what I ate for breakfast.

Monday APRIL 20

Today was a rude awakening at 6:25 in the morning. Every day Tom come's in my room and takes my diary. I hate it. We had chorus this morning. After school it snowed like crazy!! We have about 3-4 inches!! Mom was quite busy tonight.

P.S. ▓ Pray for me, I Drive!!

☺ Dawn

KEEP OUT

As the most interesting preteen on Earth, with so many precious secrets under lock and key, I had to be careful. I was absolutely convinced that my brother, Tom, was constantly trying to read my diary.

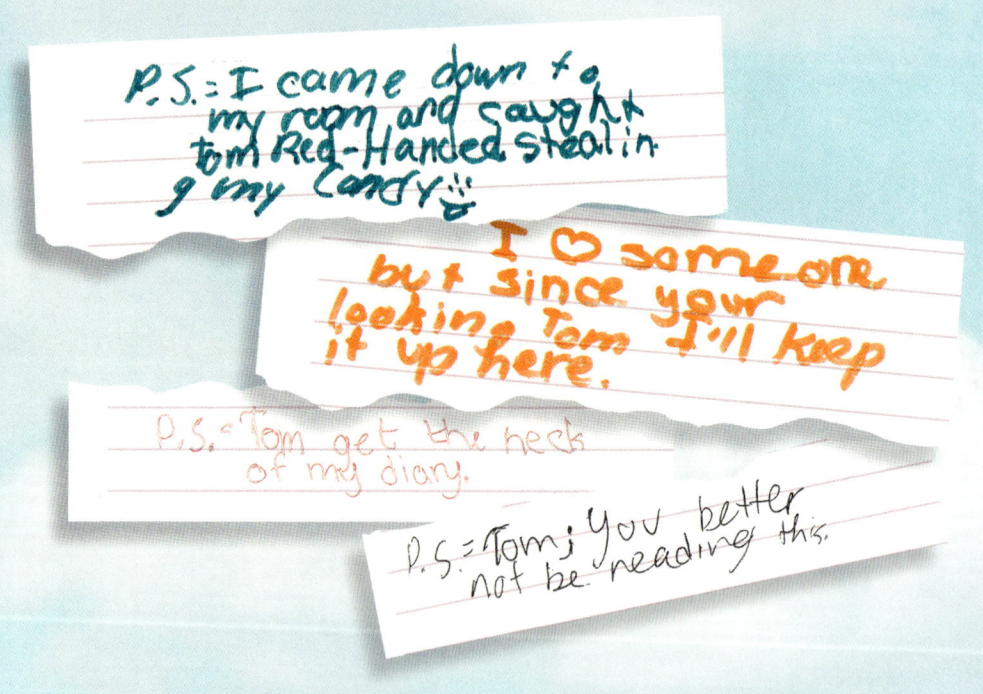

> P.S.= I came down to my room and caught Tom Red-Handed stealing my candy.

> I ♡ someone but since your looking Tom I'll keep it up here.

> P.S.= Tom get the heck of my diary.

> P.S.= Tom, you better not be reading this.

When I recently confronted him about it, here is what he had to say: "You know, I actually do think I managed to sneak a peek a few times, but after I didn't see any real dirt, I quit trying. I'm pretty sure my main goal was to annoy you, which is every big brother's duty and obligation."

KEEP OUT!!!

Chapter 5

For the most part, I got along well with my younger sister, Ginger. But given her talent, intellect, incredibly busy schedule, and ability to rock a windsuit, it was difficult not to get jealous.

On July 13, 1992, the situation with Ginger came to a head. For one sentence. With so little to go on, it's unclear what her crime was. She probably did something unforgivable, like ask me to hand her the remote.

Monday
JULY 13

Tom's game got rained out there was 2 3/4 inches of rain. I ran arons with dad this morning. Ginger acts like she's some super star and expects me to be her servant. Tonight Mom made really good potatos. We went to the movie "Sister Act" tonight.

P.S.= We love it!!
We love it!!

—Dawn

Thankfully, the arrival of some tasty tubers and Whoopi Goldberg saved the day.

Chapter 5

Being the middle child was not easy. Sometimes my greatest achievements went completely unnoticed as everyone focused on Ginger's straight-A's report card or Tom's latest asthma attack.

On January 13, 1992, for example, I wrote an amazing essay on homelessness that my teacher offered to submit to the newspaper. (Who cares that I hadn't actually ever seen a homeless person?) I couldn't wait to break the news to my parents and advise them that they should probably hire a publicist for their Pulitzer Prize–winner in the making. Their focus, however, was not on my imminent success but on finishing off the pot roast.

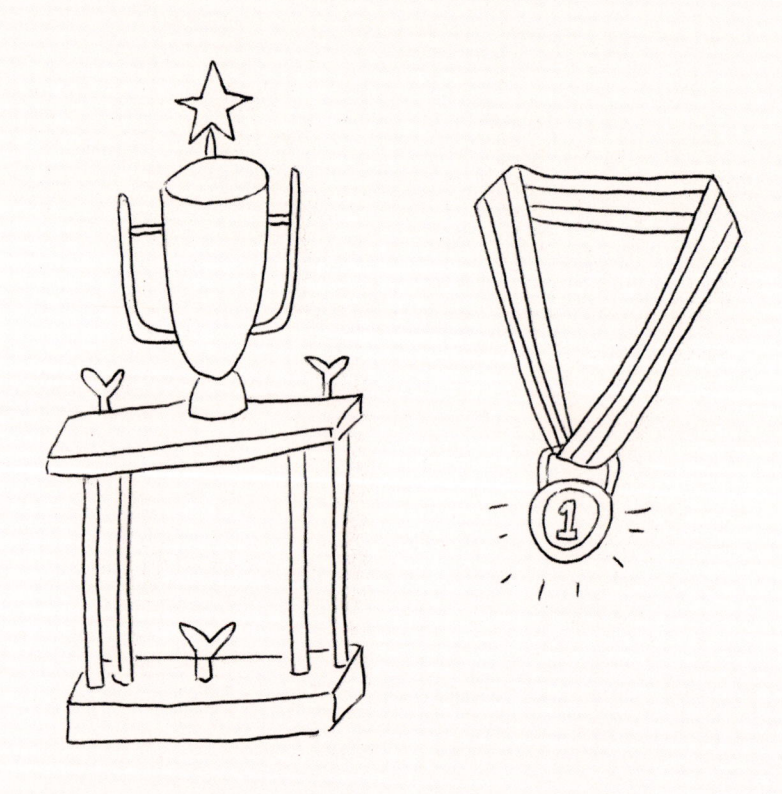

Monday
JANUARY 13

This morning I woke up at 6:30 pm!, Because I went to try out Choris. It's sort of fun! I had an o.k. lunch. At 2:00pm Tom went to get 2 teeth pulled. Ginger had Spanish after school. In reading I did A homeless essay and Mrs. Santos said she'd send it to the paper !!!!! I told my family and no one really seemed to care much. For supper we had roast.

P.S. = Grampa Luebbe is doing much better now!

Dawn

Chapter 5

The only thing worse than family drama was friend drama. While family squabbles usually only lasted a day or two and had few repercussions, friend drama could completely affect your popularity status for weeks at a time. If you were on the outs with a popular friend, you could be excluded from slumber parties, forced to move lunch tables, or, worse yet, have your chain letters go unanswered.

It is crucial for every preteen girl to know who her best friend is at all times. For me, it changed on a weekly basis. I bounced between Susanne, Jamie, Carrie, Angela, Lisa, Jeanne, and Renee. I kept careful track of my friendship rankings, as even the most minor transgression could shake up the hierarchy.

On April 21, 1990, Susanne's precarious position atop the friend pyramid grew even more tenuous as she casually disrespected my mother's job of cleaning my room. (Normally, cleaning my room was my chore, but I guess my mom must have grown fed up with my version of cleaning—shoving all my Popples and *Disney Adventures* magazines under the bed so I could get back to watching *SNICK*—and decided to tackle the mess herself.)

Susanne's careless actions would have serious consequences.

Date April, 21, 1990, Saturday.

TODAY for *breakfast* I had one piece of toast. I went outside and play Basketball. Susanne came over and played. My mom cleaned my room. Susanne messed up my room. I Don't really think Susanne is my best friend any more.
   Dawn

Apparently my reverence for breakfast earned it the coveted honor of being the only word in the entry written in cursive.

Chapter 5

There was nothing worse than having two friends who didn't like each other. Such was the case with Lisa and Jeanne.

Lisa was one of the most popular girls in school. She was super pretty, with long, permed hair and perfectly coiffed bangs. Even in third grade, she had painted fingernails and a boyfriend who was into Mötley Crüe.

Jeanne, on the other hand, was the most sophisticated girl in our class. She once showed me how to give myself a steam facial in her bathroom sink (nine-year-olds offer the best beauty advice).

I can't say if Jeanne and Lisa actually disliked each other or if it was all in my head. Whatever the case, I had to perform a delicate balancing act, hanging out with Jeanne without Lisa finding out and vice versa. I felt pressure to pick one or the other, but how was I to make this *Sophie's Choice*? If I stopped being friends with Lisa, that would mean losing my one chance at popularity. On the other hand, if I stopped being friends with Jeanne, my skin-care regimen would surely go down the tubes.

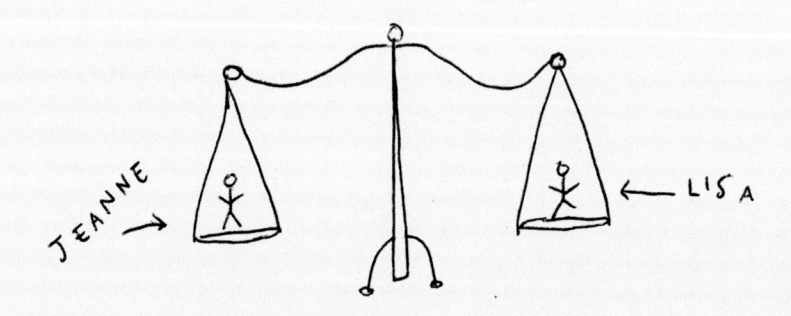

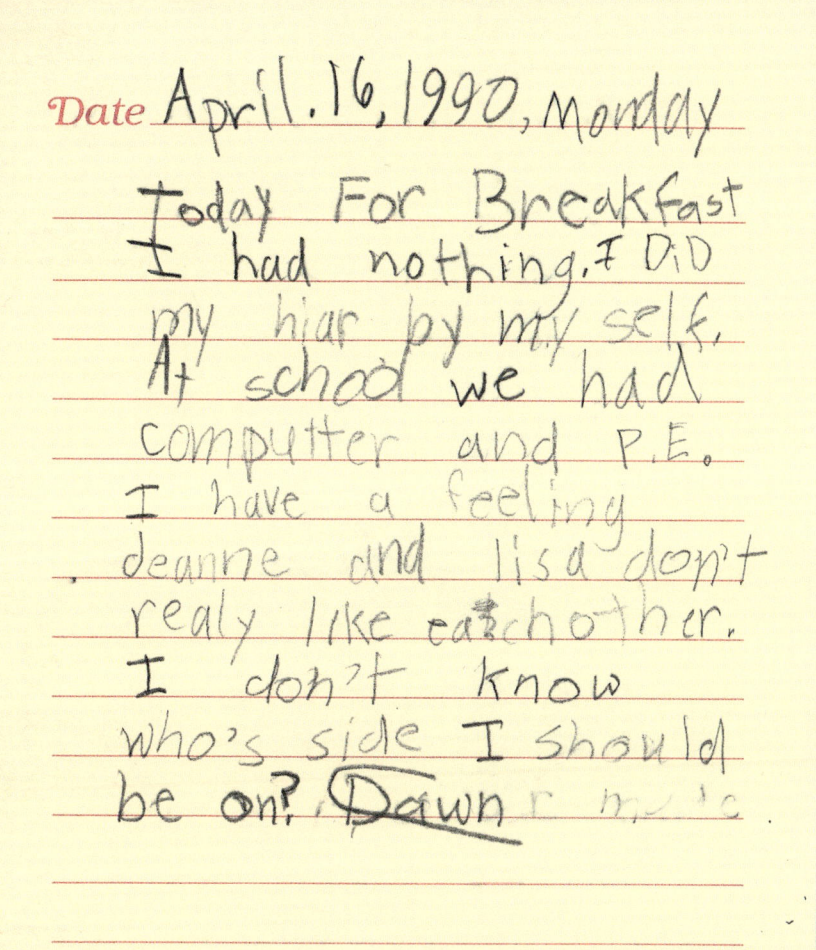

Date April. 16, 1990, Monday

Today For Breakfast I had nothing. I DiD my hiar by my self. At school we had computer and P.E. I have a feeling deanne and lisa don't realy like eachother. I don't know who's side I should be on? Dawn r m..

If only I had eaten a well-balanced breakfast, I might have been better equipped to cope with this difficult situation.

Chapter 5

The Lisa/Jeanne drama bled right into the next day. I was having a very difficult time maintaining this delicate friendship equilibrium, so much so that I had no appetite for breakfast *again*.

But Lisa's illness presented the perfect opportunity for me to sneak around behind her back, and I went with Jeanne to our school carnival, where we moseyed our way through the cakewalk and bike rally.

Our thrilling yet clandestine evening ended under the glow of the Golden Arches. Two days without breakfast works up quite the appetite. I shudder to think what Lisa might have done had she found out I was sharing a McDLT with the enemy. If only McDonald's had developed a special container to keep your friends as separate as your hamburger patty and lettuce.

Date April, 17, 1990, Tusday.

Today For Breakfast I had nothing. I did my hiar. At school we had P.E. and music. Lisa was sick Today! I played with Jeanne. I brought her to her to the calvert carnival. I also brought Jeanne to McDonalds. I wonder if lisa will be mad because I spent so much time with jeanne.
Dawn

My allegiance to my friends was as divided as the ink colors on this page.

Chapter 5

The following year, unable to handle the stress of being a double agent, I parted ways with both Jeanne and Lisa. My new best friend was Angela, who was cool for many reasons but mostly because she owned a trampoline. Everyone knows a trampoline equals instant popularity.

Things were going well in our friendship until the catastrophic events of October 15, 1991.

Oct. 15, 1991

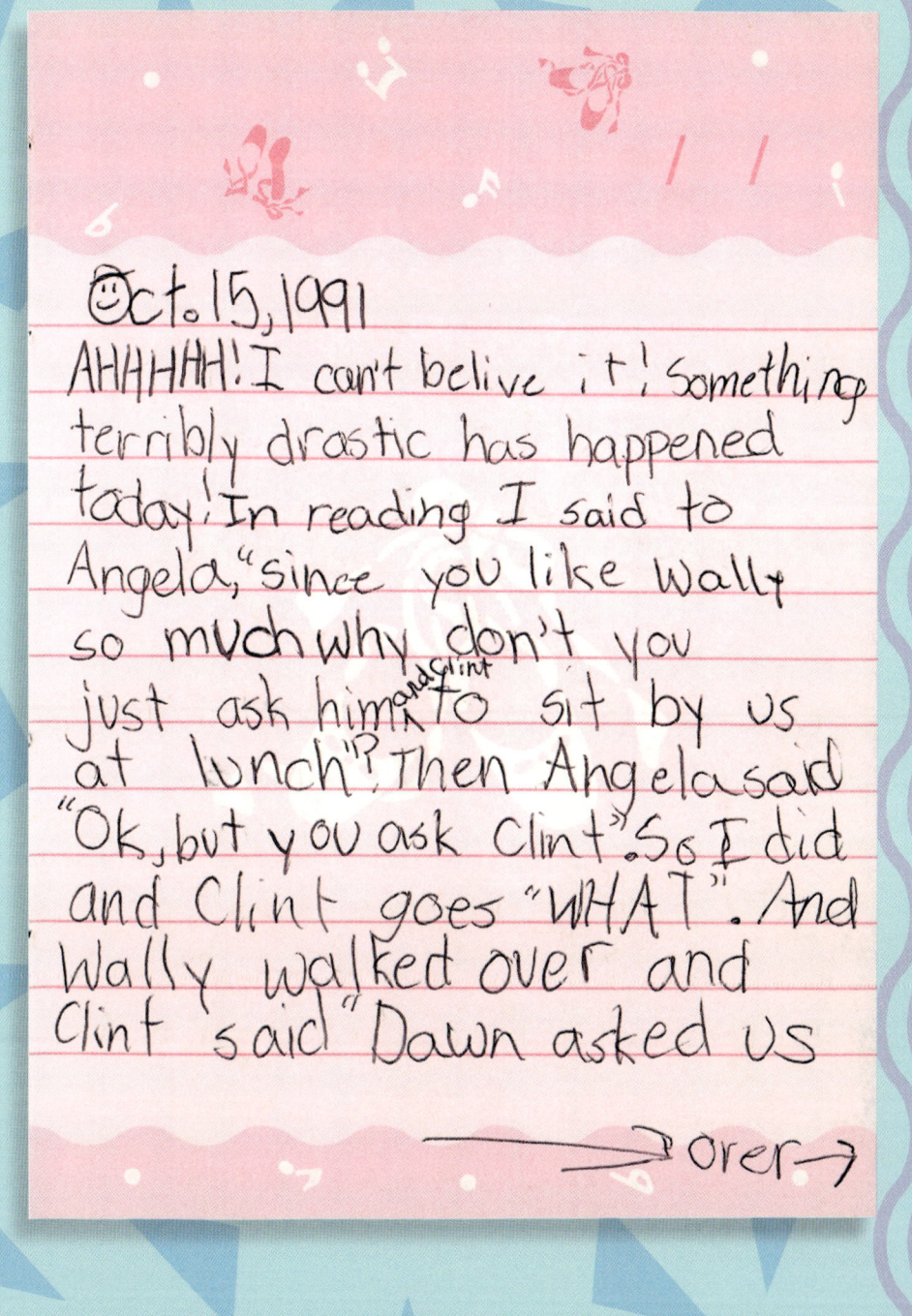

AHHHHH! I can't belive it! Something terribly drastic has happened today! In reading I said to Angela, "since you like Wally so much why don't you just ask him and Clint to sit by us at lunch"? Then Angela said "Ok, but you ask Clint". So I did and Clint goes "WHAT". And Wally walked over and Clint said "Dawn asked us

⟶ over ⟶

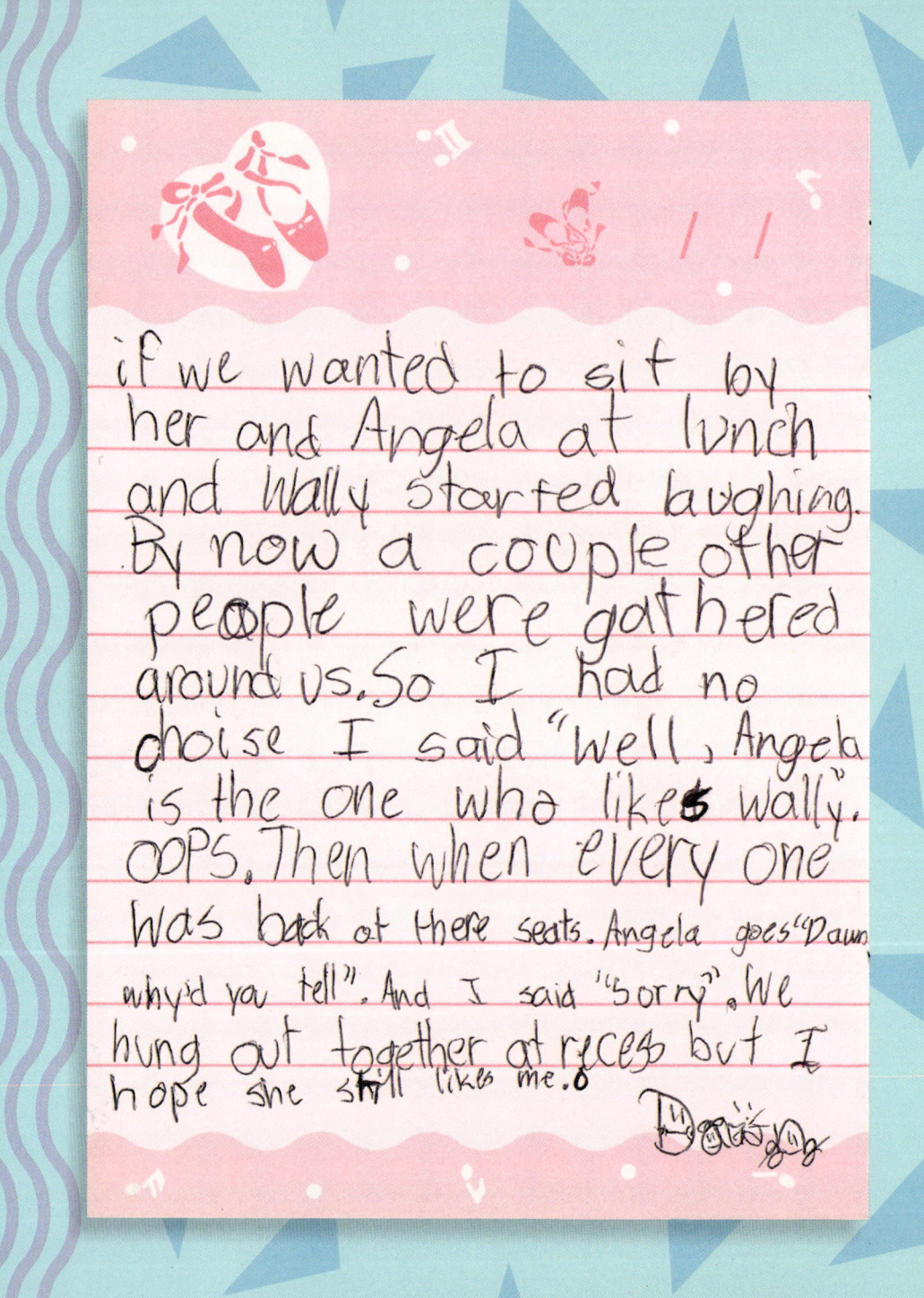

if we wanted to sit by her and Angela at lunch and Wally started laughing. By now a couple other people were gathered around us. So I had no choise I said "Well, Angela is the one who likes Wally". Oops. Then when every one was back at there seats. Angela goes "Dawn why'd you tell". And I said "Sorry". We hung out together at recess but I hope she still likes me.

Dawn

P.S. Guess what this means?

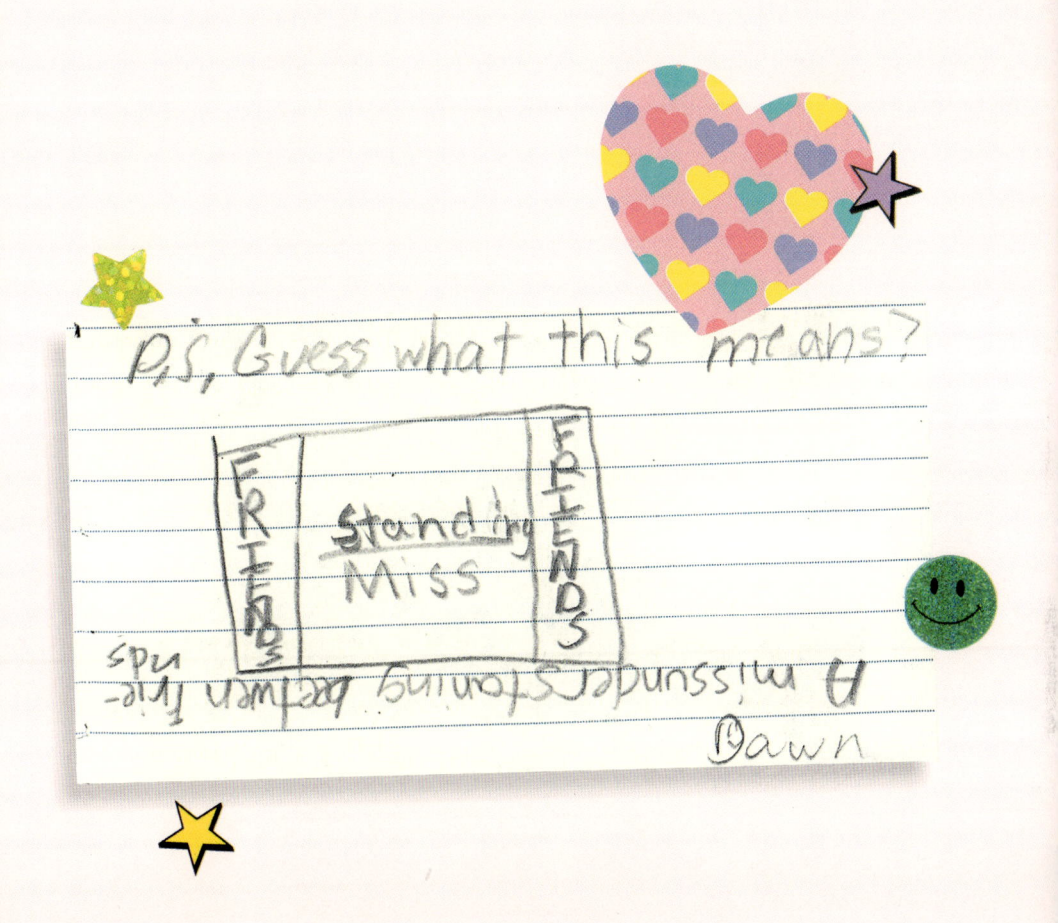

```
┌─────┬──────────────┬─────┐
│  F  │              │  F  │
│  R  │  Standing    │  R  │
│  I  │  Miss        │  I  │
│  E  │              │  E  │
│  N  │              │  N  │
│  D  │              │  D  │
│  S  │              │  S  │
└─────┴──────────────┴─────┘
```

A misunderstanding between friends.

Dawn

Chapter 6

TATO SKINS, TCBY, AND TRIX:

A Sophisticated Palate

In case you haven't noticed, rarely a day went by without my meticulously chronicling everything I ate. References to food easily outnumber any other theme or topic throughout my diaries—more than bangs, boys, and trolls combined. *Nothing* was more important. There are hundreds of sentences about food. There are two sentences about the Iraq War.

With the slow pace of my love life and my lack of achievement in, well, anything, the highlight of most days involved scoring some Teddy Grahams at lunch or Mom making spaghetti for supper.

In my 380 diary entries from 1990 to 1992, I mention specific items of food by name 370 times. Of those 370 references, only four are to fruits and vegetables.

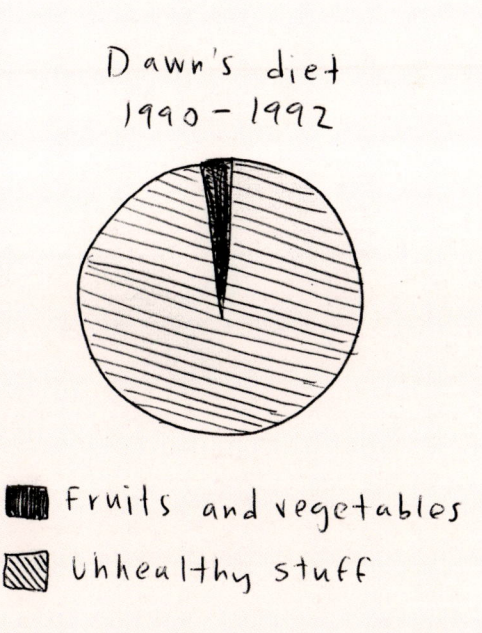

Dawn's diet
1990 – 1992

■ Fruits and vegetables
▨ Unhealthy stuff

Chapter __6__

Cookies, candy, and cake come up a lot. I had a raging sweet tooth. My true best friends during this time were ~~Angela and Jamie~~ Little Debbie, Mr. Goodbar, and Mike and Ike.

Here is my 1992 nutitional food pyramid:

A Guide to Dawn's Food Choices

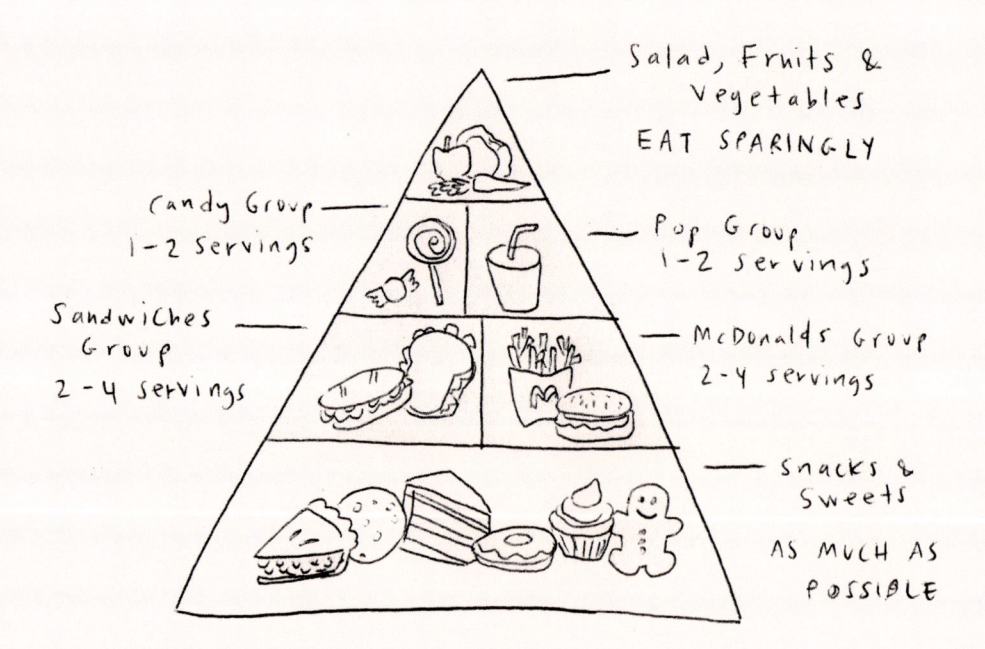

- Salad, Fruits & Vegetables — EAT SPARINGLY
- Candy Group — 1-2 servings
- Pop Group — 1-2 servings
- Sandwiches Group — 2-4 servings
- McDonalds Group — 2-4 servings
- Snacks & Sweets — AS MUCH AS POSSIBLE

When it came to beverage selection, my sweet tooth won out again. Pop was a big treat. It wasn't something we often had at home, so I was always trying to score some. Though any non-diet pop would do the trick, my preferred pick-me-ups were Cherry Coke, Dr Pepper, or, if I felt like expressing my quirky side with an off-brand beverage, OK Soda.

A couple of years later Crystal Pepsi (may it rest in peace) was my elixir of choice. With its transparent hue and Van Halen power anthem, drinking it made me feel not only like I was doing something healthy but also like I was saving the planet in the process.

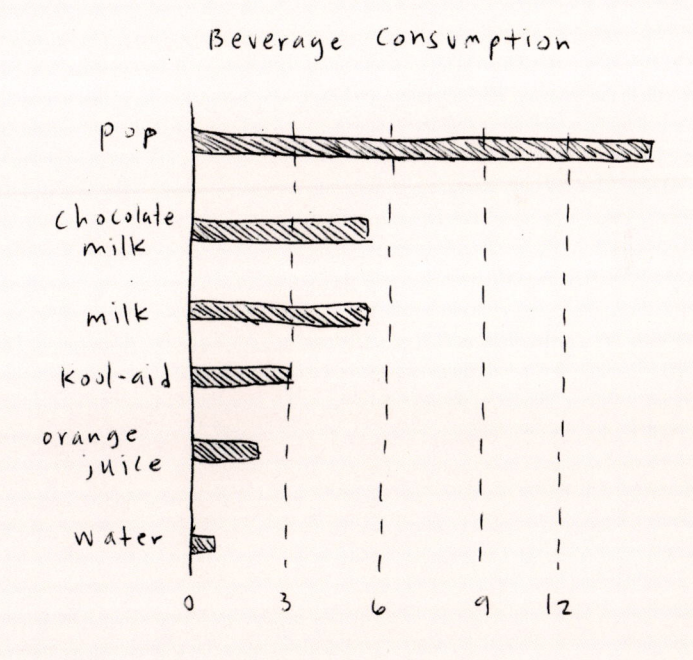

Beverage Consumption (hand-drawn bar chart)

- pop: ~13
- chocolate milk: ~4
- milk: ~5
- kool-aid: ~2
- orange juice: ~1.5
- water: ~0.5

x-axis: 0, 3, 6, 9, 12

Chapter 6

The culinary establishment I reference more than any other is McDonald's. Not only an elegant venue for many a childhood birthday gala, it was a regular pit stop en route to see the grandparents or our go-to place when Mom didn't feel like cooking. Ronald McDonald and Grimace were pretty much family, and the Hamburglar was the weird uncle I never had.

I think part of me knew I *should* eat healthier, but why have fruit when you can have a Fruit Roll-Up? Why have Corn Flakes when you can have Frosted Flakes? And, seriously, what's more fun than Fun Dip?

Date May 9, 1990, Wednsday
Today for breakfast I had candy.

Date Feb. 19, 1990, Monday,

Today for breakfast I had a ice-cream bar and gum. We did not have school Today. I watched T.V. tell lunch. For lunch we had spoggeti O's and a pop-sicle. Then we went roller skateing with Susanne. When we where at the roller skateing ring we had cotton candy AND POP! Then we came home. Then we had hot-Dogs for supper.

Dawn

This entry from February 19, 1990, shows a perfect snapshot of my typical diet. Nothing says "breakfast of champions" like a Bomb Pop and Bubble Yum. I needed these precious calories to power through my morning exercise regimen of watching *Divorce Court* and *Quantum Leap*.

After I was revitalized by a nutritious lunch and dessert, it was time for one of my favorite activities: roller-skating. Skating was *the* preteen social event in early-'90s Nebraska, and Holiday Skate World was the epicenter. Boasting colored lights, a disco ball, and cinderblock walls painted with scenes from outer space, this was our Studio 54. It was the place to be for exclusive red-carpet events like youth church outings and the quarterly School Skate.

Filled with SpaghettiOs, I had the energy to zip around the roller rink, skating with power and grace to the entire Ace of Base catalog. The only reason I took a break was to stop by the snack bar.

As a growing tween, I was mindful of what I put into my body. It was, after all, a temple—a temple filled with Lunchables and Jell-O Jigglers.

Chapter **6**

As you can tell from my realistic drawing of monochromatic, barely intertwined rings atop this entry, the 1992 Winter Olympics were in full effect.

All eyes—including those of the Luebbe household—were on Albertville, France. I watched with excitement as Kristi Yamaguchi triple Lutzed and double Salchowed her way to figure skating gold. With her infectious energy, black-and-gold sequined costume (which I couldn't help but notice bore a *very* strong resemblance to my 1992 dance recital costume), and gravity-defying bangs, who wouldn't be captivated?

So wrapped up was I in the Olympic festivities that I couldn't keep straight what we had for lunch or dinner. Luckily, I had the precious postscript to clear up any confusion.

Sunday
FEBRUARY 9

This morning I watched T.V. For lunch we had Sloppy Joes. They were better than usual. After lunch we played with Matt and Clint. Then we went to there house and watched the movie (Watcher in the Woods.) For supper we had Pork Chops.

P.S.= Correction - We had Pork Chops for lunch and Sloppy Joes for supper.

Dawn

In case you missed the Criterion Collection's release of The Watcher in the Woods, *it's a live-action Disney horror flick about two sisters who perform a séance in an abandoned chapel during a solar eclipse in an effort to bring back Karen, a teen who had been trapped in another dimension for thirty years after being crushed by a bell.*

Friday
JANUARY 3

I forgot what I had for breakfast this morning. Mom went to the YMCA today and started a slim fast diet. She had yucky tasting shakes for breakfast & lunch and she had a small dinner. This afternoon we went to see the movie "The Addams family. It was very good.

P.S.= mom has to lose 8 pounds before Jan. 20! She had these one Slim fast bars and the after-taste was like barf coming up you're throat! YUC!

Dawn

In January 1992, my mom went on a Slim-Fast diet. True to the rules set out by former Dodgers manager Tommy Lasorda, the Slim-Fast plan required having a healthy, delicious chocolate shake for breakfast, one for lunch, and then a sensible dinner, with the occasional Slim-Fast candy bar as a snack.

I found it incredibly unfair that Mom got to sit around drinking chocolate shakes and eating candy bars all day while the rest of us had to eat boring normal food. Never one to let chocolate remain in the house undisturbed, my sweet tooth got the best of me this afternoon, and I snuck into the cabinet to feast upon one of the bars. However, I quickly learned that there's a big difference between a Snickers bar and a Slim-Fast bar.

The day did have one thing going for it: an introduction to the kooky Addams clan. This movie had me thinking of following in the goth footsteps of Wednesday Addams. It was a short-lived fantasy, though, because I could never live without fuchsia.

Chapter 6

On Wednesday, June 3, 1992, the food situation in our household had turned desperate. Being "really low on good food" either meant we had run out of Shark Bites or that someone had polished off the Suddenly S'mores. Or—perish the thought—both. Would we end up like the Donner Party?

For supper, I had to get resourceful, but I managed to stay true to my religion of sugar and carbs (probably overlooking a good deal of fruits and vegetables along the way) and enjoyed a meal with scarcely an ounce of nutritional value.

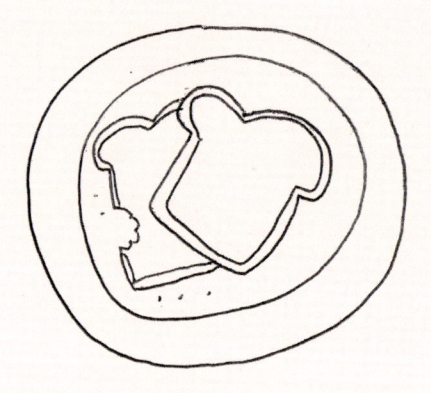

I should also mention that I religiously watched *All My Children* during the summer of '92. Never one to opt out of watching something because it was for adults, I found this show to be right up my alley. When flipping channels one day, I saw Natalie Marlowe sitting at the bottom of a well, having been thrown there by her evil twin sister, Janet Green, and I was pretty much hooked.

Wednesday
JUNE 3

Today we're really low on good food. Lunch and all sucked. I watched All my children. It was good. Opel got preagnet! Tonight we played with Clint and matt.

P.S.= I had buttered toast for supper.

Dawn

On today's episode of All My Children, *I learned that Opal Cortlandt was pregnant. A blessed day for Pine Valley, but a rather suspicious development given that Opal's husband, Palmer, was sterile.*

PRETEEN FOOD CRITIC

Ever the gourmand, I developed my food-reviewing skills early in life. With complex adjectives such as "good" and "very good," I keenly and articulately described the subtle flavors and textures of the many delicacies I had the privilege of savoring, as well as those that were simply not up to my refined level of taste.

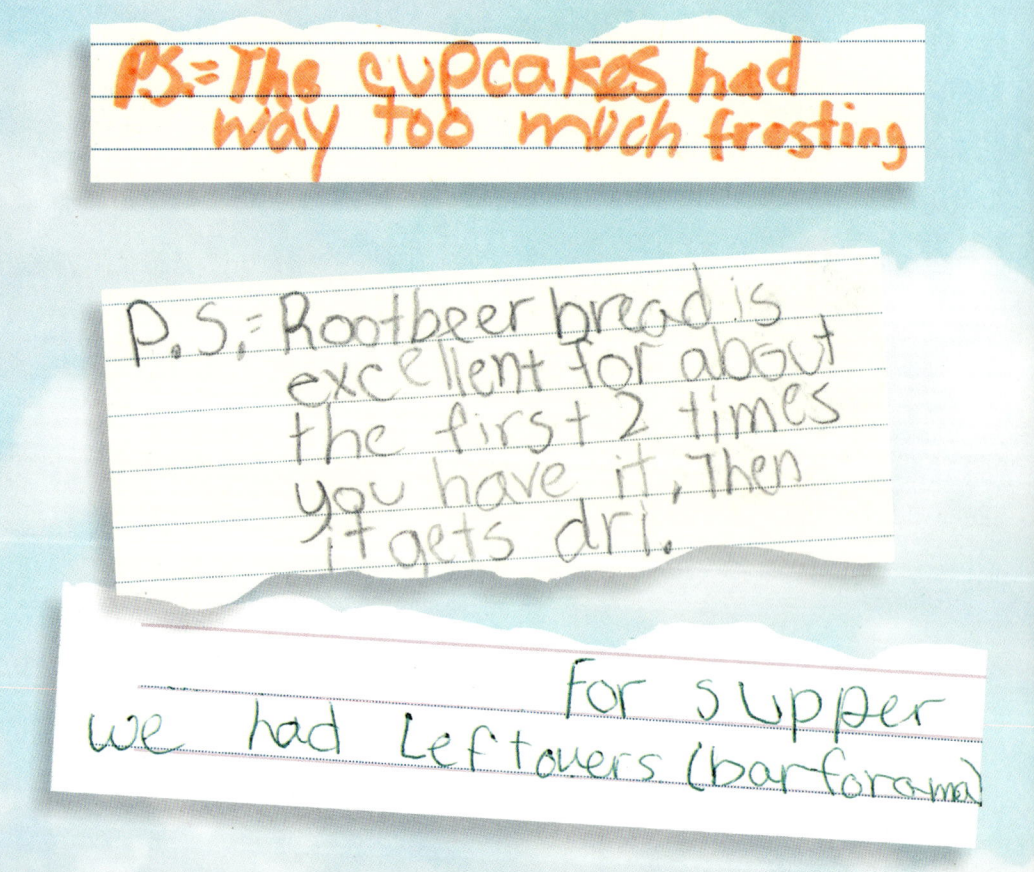

> PS= The cupcakes had way too much frosting

> P.S.= Rootbeer bread is excellent for about the first 2 times you have it. Then it gets dri.

> For supper we had Leftovers (barforama)

we had supper we had chicken. It wasn't the best.

We ate at mc-donalds. The letuce was rotten.

P.S.= The chese in the Grilled Chese sandwiches was stale!!

P.S.= I got popcorn at the Neb. game. And man Oh man does thats fill you up. I think I'll stick with malts!

supper we had speggeti. It was very very very good.

Chapter 6

This day started off the best way possible: ~~a well-balanced breakfast~~ watching Kevin Costner run around in tights. It continued swimmingly with a lunch date with my awesome grandma, who always let me order whatever I wanted. French fries and a banana split? Yes, please!

Next up: fixing screen doors with Dad. He clearly needed my help with these sorts of projects. I'm positive I did the bulk of the work while my dad sat around lazily watching.

However, by the late afternoon things went downhill quickly.

My less-than-sophisticated diet finally caught up with me. As per the postscript (in which there is certainly no amount of exaggeration), I was clearly dealing with my first bout of food poisoning.

Wednsday
JUNE 10

We got up and watched Robin Hood Prince of thiaves. Then Carries mom drae me home. & Grandma Luebbe took me out to eat. Around 2:15 I went with dad and Ginger to fix some screen doors at our old house. About 3:30 I got sick.

P.S.= Counting Today and tonight I threw up 23 times!!

— David

BORING

Some days just don't have much going for them.

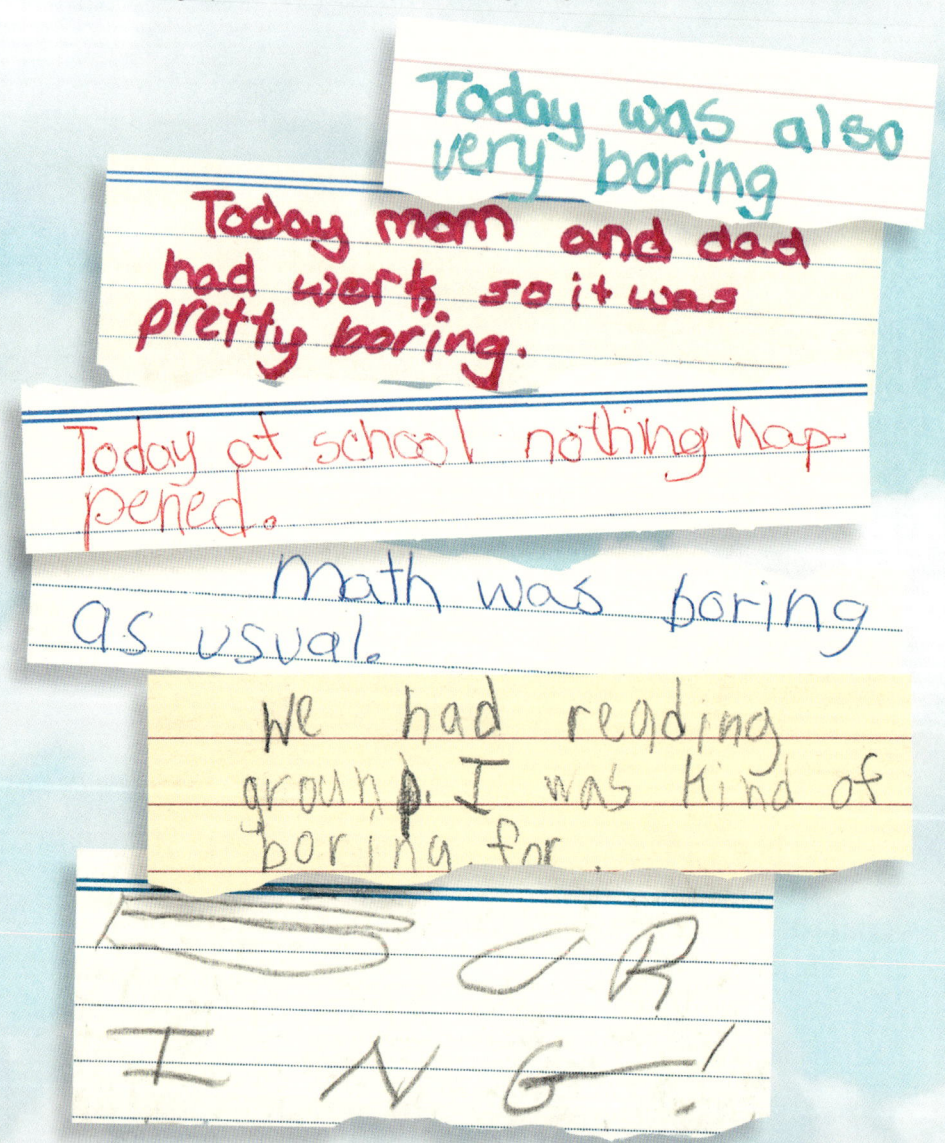

Today was also very boring

Today mom and dad had work so it was pretty boring.

Today at school nothing happened.

Math was boring as usual.

We had reading group. I was kind of boring for

BORING!

136

Chapter 7

NEBRASKA:

Horses, Tornados, and Casseroles

Chapter 7

Nebraska, in case you didn't know, is a state of great historical and cultural significance. The Cornhusker State is the birthplace of Kool-Aid *and* the popcorn ball. Duncan Hines cake mix hails from mighty Omaha, and the McRib sandwich was invented at a research lab at the University of Nebraska. As evidenced by the previous chapter, these pillars of Nebraskan history have had a profound impact on my life.

Though most of my youth was spent in cosmopolitan Lincoln, I frequently visited my grandparents' farm near Beaver Crossing, Nebraska. My siblings, cousins, and I found many productive ways to spend our time on the farm. Ever the intellectuals, we'd throw firecrackers into the cesspool of cattle waste, pretend we were *Kids Incorporated* in an abandoned dairy barn, ride the spinning cow feeder like a Tilt-A-Whirl, and race my grandpa's electric wheelchair down the gravel road until we'd get it stuck in a ditch and have to get Grandma.

Though I can't claim to be a farm girl (I was always drawn to the bright lights of Omaha), my childhood was definitely shaped by growing up in this fine state.

Eat your heart out, Waldo.

Chapter 7

Like many preteen girls, I went through a horse phase. I dreamed of being just like Brad on *Hey Dude*—a rich, beautiful girl with a boy's name who worked on a dude ranch. (If you haven't noticed, almost all my fantasies had to do with television shows.) All I needed was a French braid and some high-waisted Wranglers to transform myself into a sexy equestrian with Ted McGriff and Kyle Chandler fighting for my affection.

The closest I got to fulfilling this fantasy came in the summer of 1992, when I spent a week at a Christian horseback riding camp in Marquette, Nebraska. *Very* posh.

Despite almost no experience with horses, I enrolled in Horsemanship II, the most difficult of the riding programs. If I was going to work on a dude ranch by the time I was fifteen, I had to get on the fast track.

Tuesday
JUNE 16

Horsemanship II was lots more fun today. We trotted in the sun. We went to the waterslide today. I went down it 4 times. It was cool. I played frisbie golf. I won and Ging got 4th. Tonight a band played for us. They were good.

P.S.= No, No, my dadies not a munky.

—Dawn

I can only imagine that the postscript was a lyric from our nightly anti-evolution-themed campfire song.

Chapter 7

In addition to transforming fifth-graders into rodeo stars, the camp had a second, more important objective: to save us from eternal damnation.

Every night, following a day of trail rides, we'd gather around a campfire to hear sermons about what it meant to be "saved." Despite my regular Sunday school attendance, I was unfamiliar with the term. For me, church meant rousing games of biblical word finds, singing Amy Grant hits, and eating doughnuts. That kind of religion I could totally get behind, but this whole business of being "saved" was honestly a bit confusing. Still, sitting in the dark next to an ever-growing campfire and listening to our sixteen-year-old counselors paint a terrifying vision of hell was enough to scare even the bravest preteen into getting saved.

Although this momentous decision would be regarded by many as the most important moment of my life, I found equal spiritual fulfillment in lunch and shuffleboard.

Wednesday JUNE 17

This morning we went around barrels. Then we went on a trail ride. General would not go in water. Lunch was okay today. We played shuffleboard, it was hard. Today I accepted god in to my heart! Today we did this one safarri game. Our cabin teid for the most tokens. At campfire (bond fire) the fire got up to 12 feet! Now I'm going to bed.

P.S.= Cubby is missing!

> I don't remember who or what Cubby was. I can only assume he refused to get saved.

Chapter 7

On the last day of camp, to celebrate our victory over hell and everlasting suffering, we had a rodeo. Everyone knows that Jesus loved that sort of thing. We took turns riding around barrels in a show to end all shows.

All that hard work called for a Nebraska culinary gem: the casserole. For as long as I can remember, casseroles were a big part of my family's diet. Every holiday gathering and family reunion boasted several of these delicacies. Most casseroles had a base of Campbell's Soup and were topped with French's French Fried Onions. Such sumptuous concoctions as tuna-noodle casserole, spaghetti casserole, and hamburger-pie casserole sent my taste buds into overdrive.

On the menu this day was a mouthwatering Tater Tots casserole, something usually found only at Michelin-starred restaurants.

thursday
JUNE 18

Today is our last full day at camp. I practiced for the rodeo tomorow. I rode diamond. She did good. Lunch was super good today. It was this one tator-tot casorol. Campfire got up to about 5 feet tonight!

P.S. = wig-it-a-wig-it-a-wig-it-a WAK!!

Dawn

What better way to end a day of horseback riding and casseroles than with a lyric from that dynamic rap duo Kris Kross?

Chapter 7

For me, a weekend at my grandparents' farm was like a trip to Las Vegas. It meant unlimited pop, cookies, and the Disney Channel (a channel that, despite our constant begging, our parents wouldn't splurge for).

Grandma and Grandpa completely spoiled us, and discipline never really entered the picture. We could get away with running inside their house, having root beer floats for dinner, and watching *Dumbo's Circus* until all hours of the night with our super-fun cousin Ellie, who lived on a nearby farm.

Unfortunately, there were no horses on my grandparents' farm, but there were cows. While it's true that cows are a little less interactive than horses, this didn't stop me from playing with them or, on this day, full-on bullying them.

Date Jan. 6, 1990, Saturday.

Today for breakfast I had pancakes I only had ½ pancakes. Because I don't realy like pancakes that much. Then I got dresed. Then I watched Disney. After that Ellie came. We went outside and threw snowballs at the cows. we called the uglyest ones name moose. We put snow in grandma and grandpa's mailbox. For lunch we had nudle's. And after that I watched T.V. for supper we had hot dogs and chips. Then we went to a basket ball game Nebraska won. The score was 91 to 99. It was very very very fun. Dawn

Chapter 7

As fundamental to Nebraska as horses, cows, and casseroles is extreme weather. Tornados are, unfortunately, an all-too-regular occurrence. In school, tornado drills outnumbered fire drills and the sound of a real tornado siren was, at minimum, a biannual event

The following excerpts detail some of my encounters with stormy Nebraskan weather and conclude with the most Nebraskan of all days.

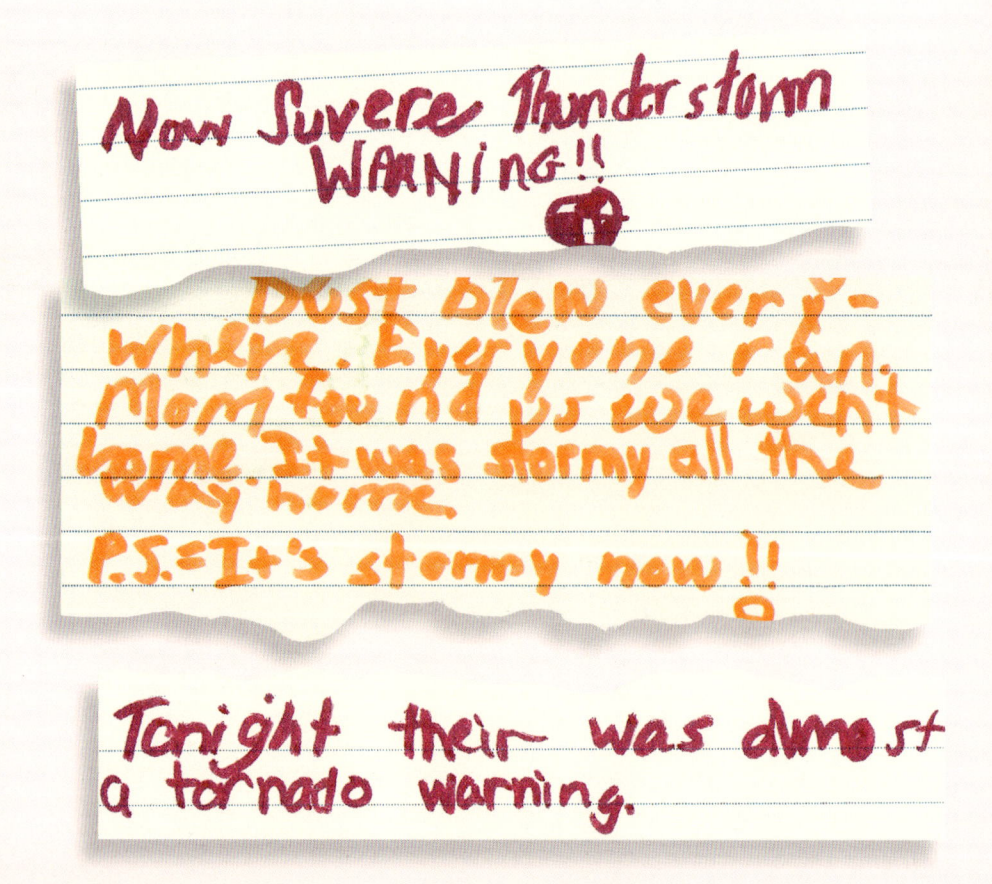

> Now Suvere Thunderstorm WARNING!!

> Dust blew everywhere. Everyone ran. Mom found us we went home It was stormy all the way home.
> P.S.= It's stormy now!!

> Tonight their was almost a tornado warning.

Thursday
AUGUST 15

Today we went horseback riding! at Timberlake ranch camp! I rode Tonia. She was a good horse but she ate to much. Then we went to Armigettin Island and had a picnic. Tonite we went to the fair on the way home it hailed marble sized hail!!! When we got back the sirens went off. We went in basement about 20 minutes.

P.S.= Then the storm was over!!

As an expert in overeating, I quickly recognized my horse's malaise.

Chapter 8

GROWING PAINS

As previously mentioned, I was a very late bloomer. Almost all my friends (including my *younger* sister) had already gotten their periods, an event that would tragically elude me until I was sixteen. At around age fifteen, I started seriously wondering if there was something my parents had neglected to tell me.

I had a flat chest, a sea of freckles, and a figure that most closely resembled a young Larry Bird.

Consequently, I had no need for things like deodorant, a bra, or a razor until well into college. But I would rather have missed a whole season of *90210* than be the only fifth-grader at Humann Elementary without these feminine staples.

I was under the impression that if I acquired these things, it would help the process of puberty along. If I wore a bra, certainly my boobs would grow into it. If I applied Teen Spirit, I'd exude the heady perfume of a mature woman. If I used a maxi pad, I'd get my period. This was my *Field of Dreams* approach to becoming a woman.

Thursday
MAY 21

This morning there was no band. We played softball in Phs Ed. my team is winning 9 to 2. Lunch was fine today!!!!!!! After school there was no dance. We went to get Tom's shot. We got cookies. I had to wash dishes. Ginger had Gymnastics. I shaved my legs tonight for the first time.

P.S.- I didn't do that well!!

Dawn

Nothing calls for seven exclamation points like a mediocre lunch.

In the fifth grade all my friends started shaving their legs. Pretty much overnight having hairless legs became as important as having a Caboodle.

I clearly remember the moment I realized I was the only girl who had not leaped over this crucial preteen hurdle. I was in science class and we had broken into discussion groups to talk about *The Voyage of the Mimi*. Due to the warm spring weather, everyone in my all-girl group was wearing shorts.

Instead of discussing the diet of humpback whales and how to create freshwater on a desert island (essential knowledge for any Midwestern kid), my group talked about shaving—how often they shaved, whether they stood up or sat down. I sat cross-legged and leaned forward, stealthily pulling my oversize D.A.R.E. T-shirt down over my unshaven legs. That night I pledged to do something about it.

I was way too embarrassed to ask my mom to buy me a razor, so I took matters into my own hands. After school I sat on my carpeted bedroom floor with my dad's freshly stolen razor and shaving cream and went to work, plowing through the blond peach fuzz on my legs. It never occurred to me to use water.

This rogue method (duly summed up in the postscript) produced rather patchy and razor-burned results. Upon surveying the hack job on my legs, I meekly hid the pilfered razor in my underwear drawer, waited several months, and eventually asked my mom to provide some proper tools and instruction.

Chapter 8

Another important step to becoming an adult is wearing deodorant. For months I longed to wear it—ever since it was the primary topic of conversation at Angela's slumber party.

As luck would have it, one day my mom came home from the grocery store with deodorant for both Ginger and me. And it wasn't just any deodorant; it was Teen Spirit Pink Crush, the deodorant made specifically for *teenage* armpits. I felt very sophisticated, being only eleven and wearing a product with "Teen" in the title. The first few weeks, I applied it several times a day, because my daily activities of napping and television watching really worked up a sweat.

Sunday
APRIL 5

Today we went to a kite flying contest with the kites we made. It was really fun. Ellie came home with us to G&G Luebbe's. Mom picked us up soon. Mom bought us deoderent. Ginger acted so excited.

P.S. = do dee

Dawn

Notice how I mock Ginger for expressing the very same excitement that I felt myself.

Chapter 8

Adding to the year's landmark events, ~~Bill Clinton was elected president~~ I got my first bra. I wouldn't actually need one for close to a decade, but that didn't dampen my excitement or my terror at the thought of my brother finding out.

The momentous purchase took place the day before we left for a family vacation to Los Angeles. I had never been to California before. Everything I knew about it I had learned from *90210* and my cool namesake, Dawn, in The Baby-sitters Club books. These highly reliable references led me to believe that California was a state that only allowed the most mature and good-looking people to enter (to be fair, I still live under this assumption).

With my new training bra, I was ready to hit the Hollywood Walk of Fame, Universal Studios, and Disneyland (the go-to places of all mature adults).

Thursday JULY 23

Today around 11:34 me, mom, and Ginger went to Gateway. We ate at Food Quart. Then we went to Lorrie Kennel's for dresses. Then we went to Target, me and Ginger got new bras. We packed tonight. Cause tomorrow were going to L.A.

P.S= Tom; You better not be reading this.

DAWN

I was a new woman. Not only was I wearing a bra, I was also experimenting with semicolons.

Chapter 8

March 6, 1992, was that equally dreaded and anticipated day in the fifth grade during which boys went to one classroom and girls to another for a very special conversation.

In the girls' room, the petite and friendly Mrs. Decker told us all about periods and showed us a terrifying object called a tampon. We then watched a video about a girl who gets her period and her mom bakes her a cake. With the expectation that cake crowned the whole event, I became all the more eager for the big day.

Exactly what happened in the boys' room was a big mystery and a prime topic of conversation among us girls. Utilizing their best clinical vocabulary, Angela said they were talking about boners while Lisa argued they were talking about humping. But I had my own theory that the ultra-hip, smoking-hot Mr. Sidel put on Aerosmith and taught the boys how to grow stubble.

Friday
MARCH 6

Today in school we got separated. Boy's in Mr. Sidel's room, & Girl's in Mrs. Decker's room. We talked 'bout Pouberty & got booklets in stuff. After school I cleaned bathrooms & watched T.V.

P.S.: We stuck a sign on dad's back that said "wide load". He didn't find it!!

Dawn

> *I should note that my dad is, and has always been, a rather thin person.*

Chapter 8

Getting my period was a top priority. A couple of my friends had already gotten theirs, and they were automatically set apart from the rest of us. No doubt these worldly and sophisticated women secretly dined on caviar, read *Vanity Fair*, and summered in the Hamptons. Little did I know, the special event marking womanhood wouldn't happen to me until almost five years after this entry.

The only thing more embarrassing than not having your period was having your mom and your sister talk about it behind your back. It was bad enough that my younger sister had already had her period for years. Did they have to go talking about when I'd get mine?!

At least the night started off well. I mean, what movie could possibly be more appropriate for an eleven-year-old girl's birthday party than one with Scott Bakula and Sinbad playing college football?

Oct. 14, 1991

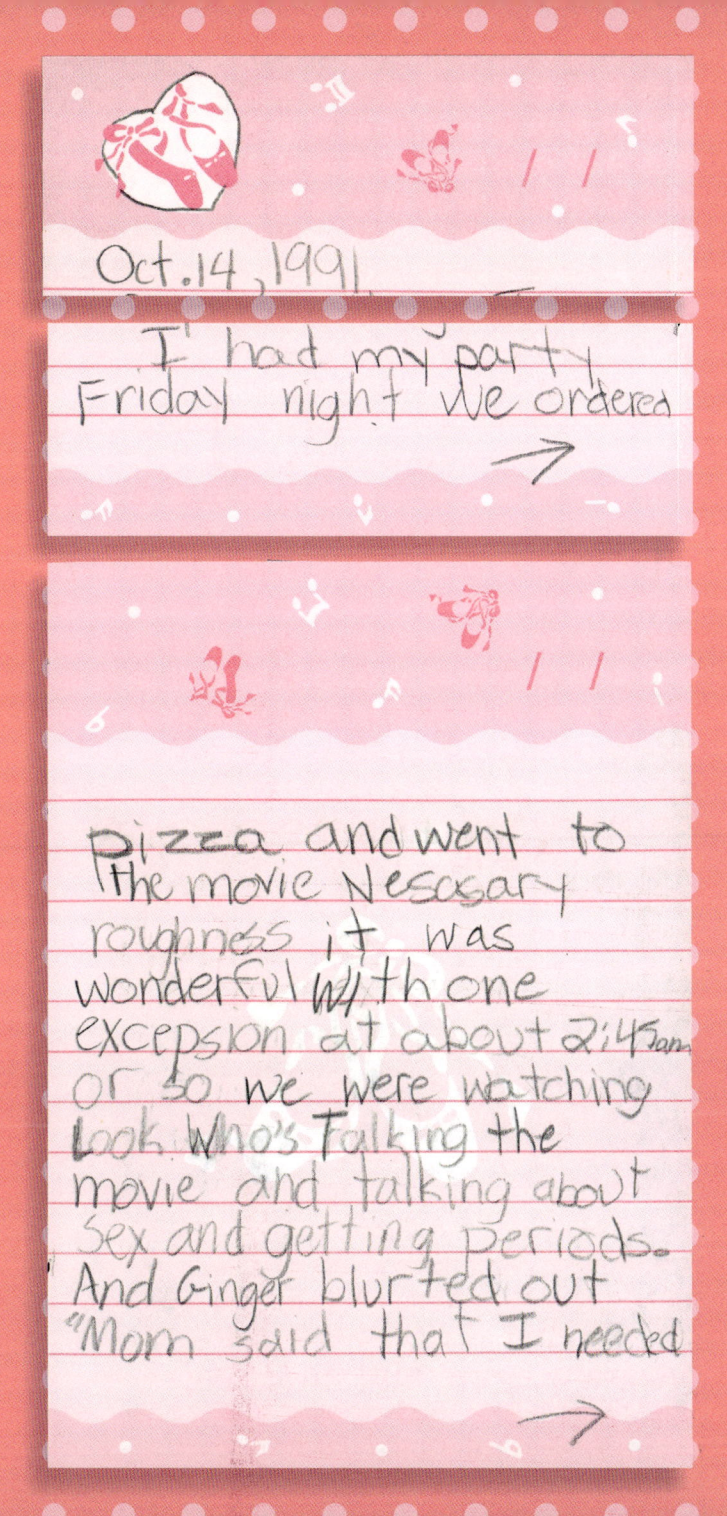

I had my party Friday night we ordered →

pizza and went to the movie Nesesary roughness it was wonderful with one excepsion at about 2:45am or so we were watching Look who's Talking the movie and talking about sex and getting periods. And Ginger blurted out "Mom said that I needed

→

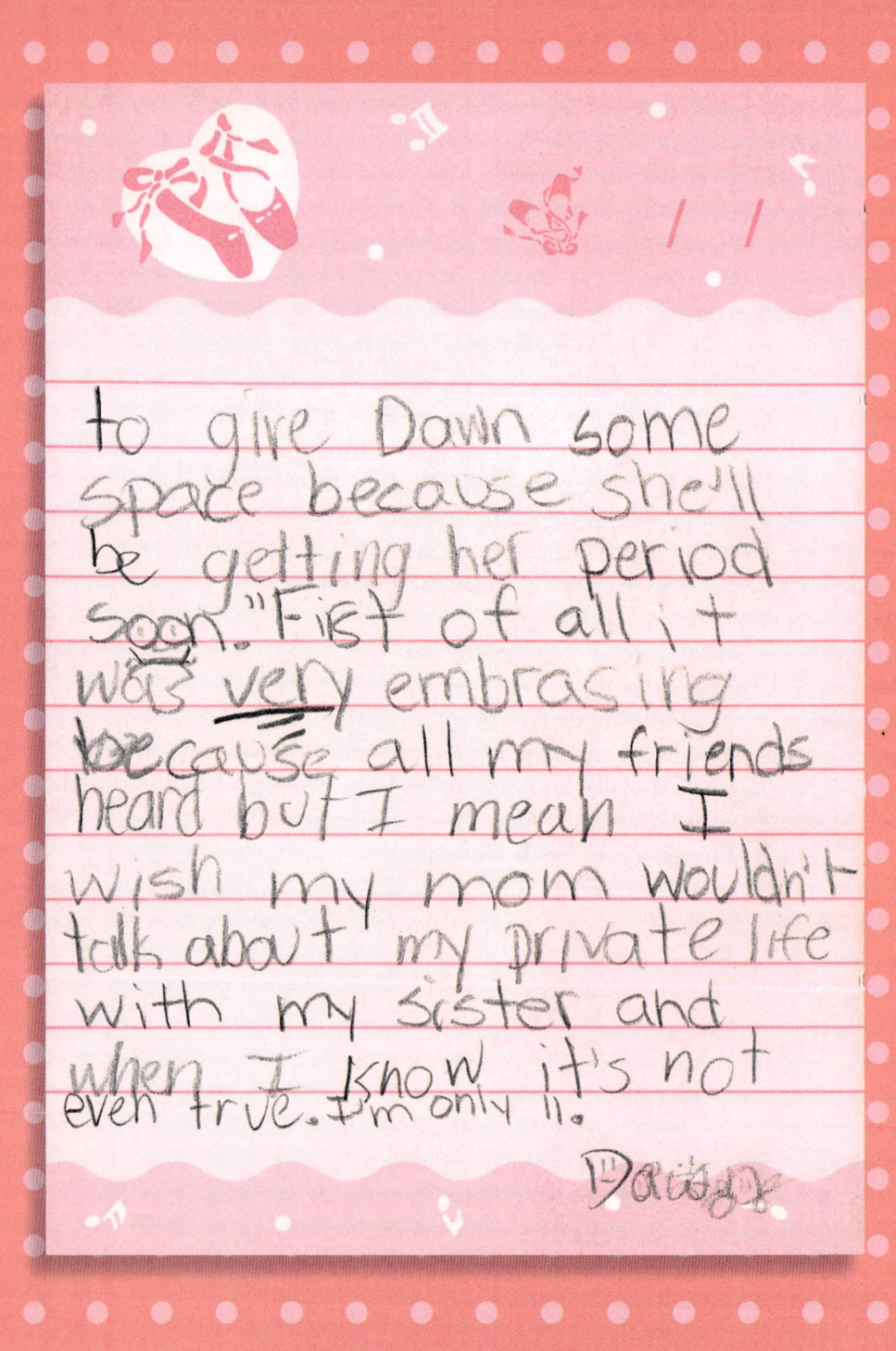

to give Dawn some space because she'll be getting her period soon." Fist of all it was very embrasing because all my friends heard but I mean I wish my mom wouldn't talk about my private life with my sister and when I know it's not even true. I'm only 11.

Daisy

PRIVATE PROPERTY

Chapter 8

The important event marking womanhood, that precious day when I got my period, finally came in 1996 when I was sixteen. It did not, however, happen in the way that Mrs. Decker's video showed us. For starters, it didn't involve cake.

Our family had just taken in a Brazilian foreign exchange student, Christiana, and it was her first night in town. Ginger and I decided that the best way to welcome anyone to America was to take them to see Gallagher perform at the Nebraska State Fair.

Seated next to a very confused, non-English-speaking Christiana, I laughed uproariously as Gallagher used his Sledge-O-Matic to crush everything from eggs to iceberg lettuce to, of course, watermelons.

It was after this amazing finale that I went to the bathroom of the Bob Devaney Sports Center and realized that my dream had come true. I had become a woman in the presence of a balding prop comic.

Had I known it was this simple, I would have splurged for tickets when Gallagher played Des Moines back in '92.

With my Cancun shirt and windswept bangs, I'm eagerly awaiting the opening of Señor Frogs, Lincoln.

THE EVOLUTION OF THE SIGNATURE

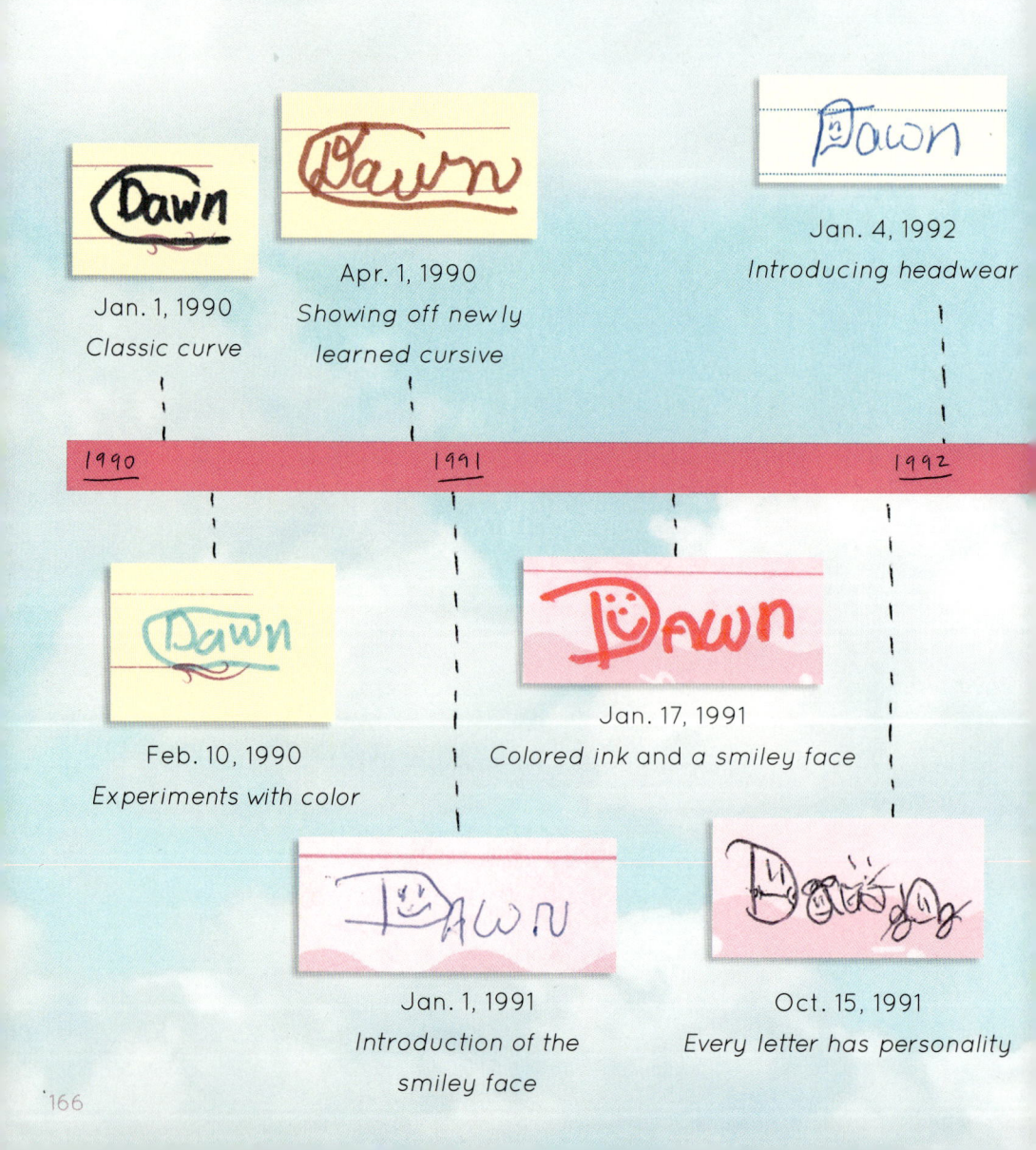

Jan. 1, 1990
Classic curve

Apr. 1, 1990
Showing off newly learned cursive

Jan. 4, 1992
Introducing headwear

1990 — 1991 — 1992

Feb. 10, 1990
Experiments with color

Jan. 17, 1991
Colored ink and a smiley face

Jan. 1, 1991
Introduction of the smiley face

Oct. 15, 1991
Every letter has personality

Mar. 11, 1992
Graphic tornado

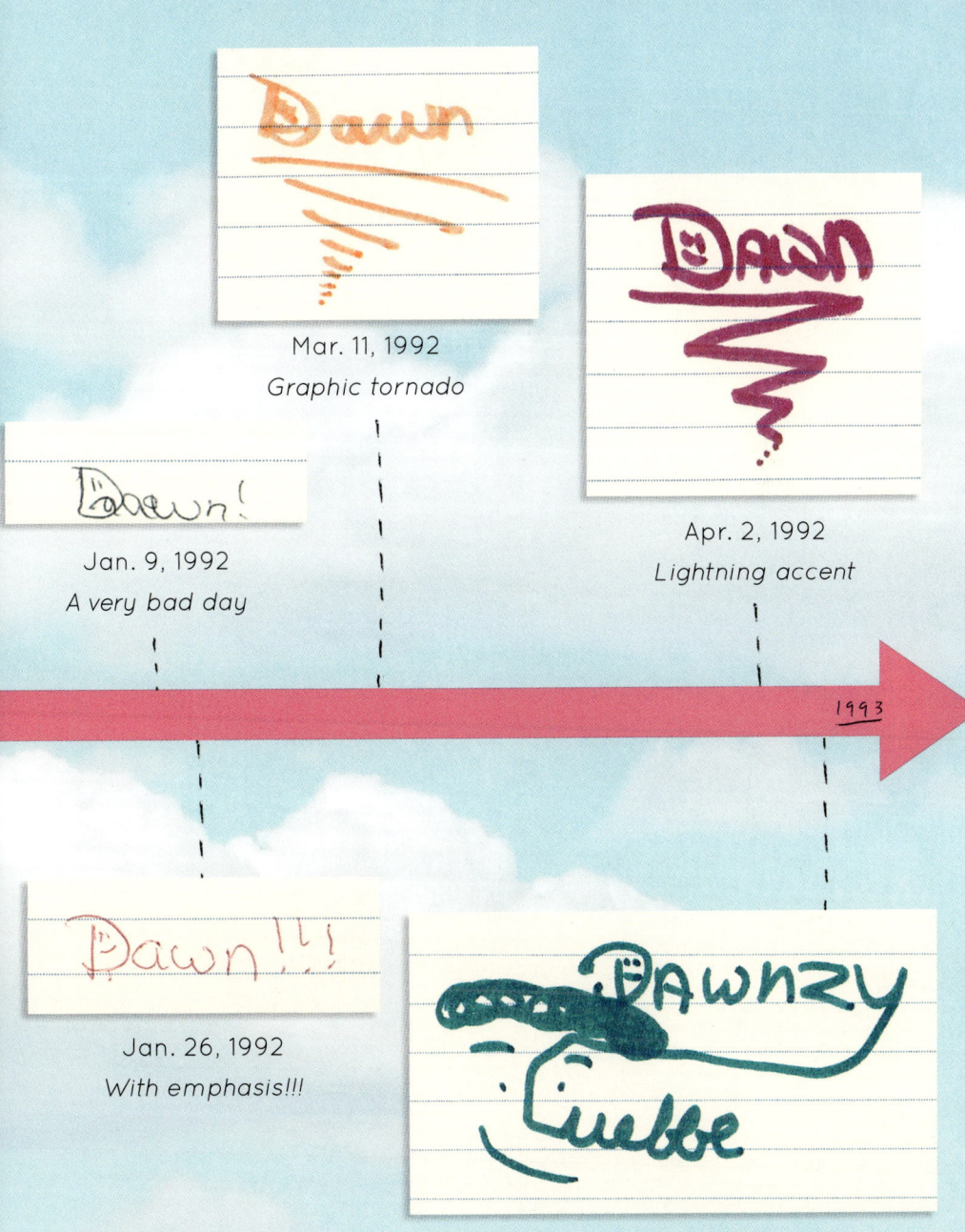

Apr. 2, 1992
Lightning accent

Jan. 9, 1992
A very bad day

1993

Jan. 26, 1992
With emphasis!!!

Apr. 6, 1992
The signature takes over

EPILOGUE

A lot has changed since 1992. *Beverly Hills, 90210* got canceled, Kirk Cameron got married, and I finally grew my bangs out (sorry, Mom). But there are also a lot of things that have stayed the same: John Stamos's hair, my cake consumption, and my mom's divine fashion sense (her denim jumpsuit is more popular than ever).

I still think about Dan sometimes and wonder what he's up to. Does he still play four square? Does he still wear big sweaters? Has he made any new banners lately?

Though I long ago left Nebraska, I still enjoy casseroles, get excited at the threat of extreme weather, and was at the opening day of Manhattan's first Dairy Queen (it's about time!).

I have continued keeping a diary on and off since the early '90s. And I can honestly say, the only thing that makes me cringe more than my 1992 diary is my 2002 diary:

> 2-12-02
> He winks more than anyone I've ever met.
> But with him it's not at all sexual or bizarre.
> It's just part of him.
> Like bad coffee in New York City deli's
>   in those blue cups with foreign writing.
> It works for him, naturally.

At least my spelling had improved, "thos" excepted.

I wish I could say that in the last twenty years I outgrew my awkwardness. But, truth be told, my glasses are thicker, my long-limbed dancing still incites cringing, and clothes just aren't made for my 6' 2" frame.

But despite these generally awkward attributes, I really don't feel awkward anymore. The other day I was having dinner with a friend and bragging about my current state of self-acceptance and coolness. She kept trying to interject, but I wouldn't let her, rushing to explain my breakthrough. Unable to get a word in between my boasts, she finally pointed at my shirt. I looked down and saw three spaghetti noodles stuck there that had long since dried.

They'd been there for hours.

I went home and wrote about it in my diary.

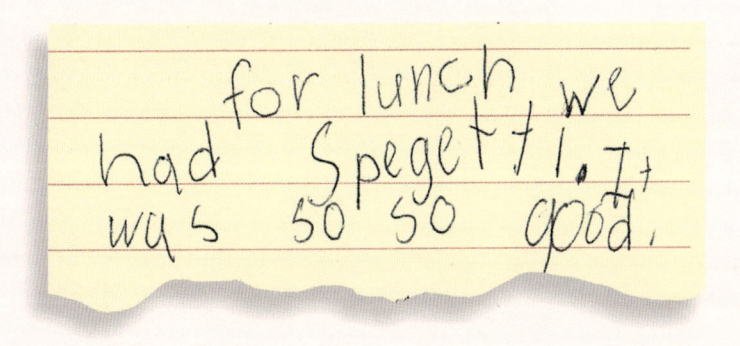

> had for lunch, we
> Spegetti. It
> was so so good.

GLOSSARY

Affectionate: efectionet

"Bohemian Rhapsody": Moheamian RapCity.

Broke: brock

Bruise: Broose

Camp: kamp

Casserole: casorol.

Cinnamon: cinamen

Choir: Quier

Chorus: quoros

Ditz: dits

Does: dose

Dry: dri.

Errands: arons.

Fruit: Froot

Gruesome: groosome

Lasagna: lazonya

Meatball: meetball

Monkey: munky.

Neighbor: naibor

Necklace: necholas

Ouija: weegee

Practiced: parkticed

Puberty: pouberty

Venice: venes

ACKNOWLEDGMENTS

I'd like to thank my parents and Tom and Ginger for allowing me to publish these embarrassing stories and pictures of them. I can assure you, they are all very cool and attractive people now.

I'd also like to thank Nolan and Dan for contributing pictures and putting up with my creepy stalking (then and now). Also a big thanks to Sarah for supplying that incredible bangs portrait.

I'd like to thank my agent, Kent D. Wolf, and editor, Samantha Weiner, for their tremendous help in putting this book together and reminding me about important '90s staples such as *Star Search* and *The Face on the Milk Carton*. And a huge thank you to Rachel Willey for helping capture the essence of the '90s through her design.

I want to thank all of the readers of my Tumblr, without which this book would not have been possible.

A number of friends provided invaluable feedback; in particular, Casey Muratori, Susannah Bohlke, Mark Rosenberg, Margaret Miller, Onassis, Ginger Gloystein, and especially my incredible husband, Jeff Roberts. He is a HUNK!

ABOUT THE AUTHOR

Dawn Luebbe is a Los Angeles–based actor and comedian, and the creator of the Tumblr blog www.my1992diary.com. She is a regular performer at the Upright Citizens Brigade Theatre and has performed with sketch group Onassis at comedy festivals around the country, including San Francisco Sketchfest, Austin's Out of Bounds, and New York Comedy Festival. She has appeared in comedy shorts for CollegeHumor, IFC, NickMom, and UCB Comedy. Dawn holds a BFA from New York University's Tisch School of the Arts.

Her diet still consists primarily of cookies.

Photo credit: Ari Scott

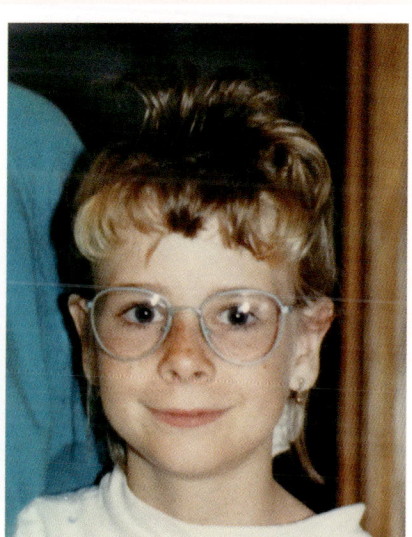

P.S.= that's the story.

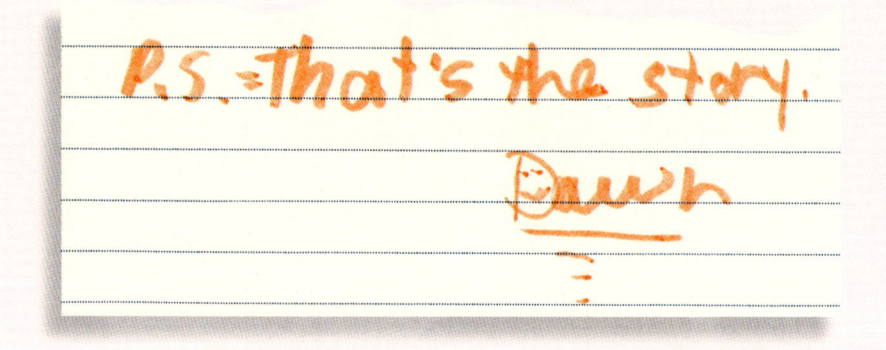

Dawn

New Year's Resolution = to finish this Diary.

Nick Names... Pasta Queen, Dawnzy, & Electra and full nick Name is... Dawnzy Electra Elizabeth Hey you Luebe

Favorite Food..... Spegetti!

Favorite color.... Purple

Favorite instrument: Clarinet ♪♫𝄞#

Siblings... Tom Luebbe & Ginger Gloystein

Favorite subjects... Art & Reading

Cats we've had:: April, Bleu, Hershey, & Tyson

Best Friends: Ginger, Angela, Carrie, Andrea, Stephanie, & Reene, SUSANNE, Jami Jo

Favorite song group C&C Music Factory

Hobbies: Art, (crafts), Water skiing, Dancing, sleeping,

COOL!

Photo credit: Morgan Dubin